DUSTOFF 7-3

Saving Lives under Fire in Afghanistan

by
Erik Sabiston

"…what makes the story so special isn't the details of those days—the shark-toothed terrain, thin air, and thinner margins—but the weirdly pedestrian nature of it all. The Army air ambulance corps is the only fully equipped emergency fleet in the military, and heroism is inscribed in its basic job description. Its helicopters are on the front lines of a parallel war effort, a mission not to take lives but to save them—and, almost unbelievably, it's a mission that's working."

—Newsweek

I expected adrenaline junkies or war cowboys, but instead found four regular people susceptible to the same fears and doubts as anyone else.

Tony Dokoupil— *NBC News*

Absolutely incredible.

Charlie Rose—*CBS News*

DUSTOFF 7-3

Saving Lives under Fire in Afghanistan

by
Erik Sabiston

WARRIORS PUBLISHING GROUP
NORTH HILLS, CALIFORNIA

Dustoff 7-3: Saving Lives under Fire in Afghanistan

A Warriors Publishing Group book/published by arrangement with the author

The views presented are those of the author and do not necessarily represent the views of the Department of Defense (DOD), its components, or its personnel.

PRINTING HISTORY
Warriors Publishing Group edition/May 2015

ISBN 978-0-9897983-6-5

Library of Congress Control Number 2015930637

The name "Warriors Publishing Group" and the logo
are trademarks belonging to Warriors Publishing Group

PRINTED IN THE UNITED STATES OF AMERICA

10 9 8 7 6 5 4 3 2 1

For Tess

In memory of:

SFC Jared Monti
SSG Patrick Lybert
SPC Brian Bradbury
SSG Heathe Craig
1LT Dimitri del Castillo
SGT Nigel Kelly
SPC Kevin Hilaman
CPL Angelo Vaccaro

PROLOGUE

I AM NOT A HERO. I believe what a Green Beret once told me: all the heroes he knew were buried at Arlington. The last time I met a Green Beret, he was riding in the back of our medevac helicopter, his right eye having been blown out that morning. He sat on the floor with a huge, bloody bandage wrapped over his head and under his scraggly beard. He refused all pain medicine. He was laughing and joking. Whatever place we had picked him up from seconds earlier was a place so terrible to him that getting out of there alive—even after losing an eye—made that day the best day of his life.

I get paid to pick people up on the worst day of their lives. The day they scream for their Mom, the day they thrash against agonizing pain and face eternity alone, thousands of miles from the very people that they got out of bed for that morning. Just before we flew them out, every one of them imagined that they'd live to see their grandkids grow up. I have to fly as fast as I can, but I can't fly fast enough. I can still see their faces, clenched in agony and desperation, and then the shock as their eyes widen and their skin pales to a sickening fish-belly white. They see through me. I am the chariot driver that takes them to their death.

I know what that Green Beret meant about heroes buried at Arlington. So when I look at the November 12th edition of Newsweek magazine, I see a fraud depicted in the featured article. A banner headline on the cover declares it's "The Heroes Issue" and those words run right across my chest. In the cover photo, two members of my helicopter crew stand on either side of me in our flight gear as we stare into space.

The photographer kept asking us to think about the mission while we stood there uncomfortably for what seemed like forever. All I could think about was that Sergeant Julia Anne Bringloe should have been there with us. Without my flight medic, it was an empty moment. If anything, she should have been on the cover by herself. And I should not have been there at all. I'm no hero—but I do fly heroes to a hospital. Or on the first leg of their journey to the grave.

Not everybody who fights in combat is a hero.

Not every hero in a war fights.

This story is for heroes.

CHAPTER 1: ALONE

Not for fame or reward, nor lured by ambition or goaded by necessity, but in simple obedience to duty.
—Inscription on a headstone at Arlington National Cemetery

The Kunar Valley, Afghanistan
21 June 2006

"THAT'S MY GUY. I'm gonna get him," Staff Sergeant Jared Monti shouted to the sniper hunkered down at his shoulder. His eyes were fixed on his wounded comrade. He tossed his radio at the man and started to move. "You're Chaos 3-5 now!"

Monti surveyed the situation on the battlefield with a growing sense of horror. More than 50 Taliban fighters had ambushed his team. The Taliban knew where they'd be, tipped off by watching yesterday's resupply mission. And now one man was dead and others seriously wounded. The most pressing problem was Private First Class Brian Bradbury, hit by shrapnel from a rocket-propelled grenade and lying motionless on his stomach in the open, just a few meters from where Monti crouched behind cover. Bradbury was close, but the Taliban was shooting at anything that moved on this bad day in the mountains of eastern Afghanistan, so reaching him was going to be difficult and dangerous. Bradbury was badly hurt and terrified, but he couldn't move. It was almost suicide for anyone to try and reach him. Staff Sergeant Monti knew that—and he also knew he had to try.

As his soldiers laid down a barrage of covering fire, Monti dove into the open and headed for the wounded man. He was driven back to cover twice with bullets tearing up the ground and whistling past his head. On his third try to reach his friend, Monti made better progress, dodging and ducking through scrabble and battlefield debris. He nearly made it, but the Taliban saw what was happening and directed a barrage of RPGs and small arms at both men out there in the open. There was a scream of pain and then all the other survivors of the ambush realized they had another casualty.

As Monti lay bleeding next to Bradbury, the air support he'd called for finally arrived overhead. Two attack jets dove on the Taliban positions, dropping bombs that landed just a few hundred yards from the battered infantry unit. Shrapnel obliterated treetops and smoking slivers of blasted wood fell all around the grunts that huddled in place, hoping the bombs would either kill the Taliban or drive them out of the area. The ordnance was falling so close that the detonations nearly deafened them and threatened to loosen teeth. Those that were brave enough to take a quick peek saw waves of fire consuming the hillside where the Taliban had dug in to spring their ambush.

And then it was over. The jets disappeared, and so did the Taliban. Darkness began to descend on the Kunar Valley. The soldiers broke cover to deal with their wounded and dead. The only chance for the wounded now was a Medevac helicopter. Dustoff would come. They always did.

At Jalalabad Air Base, most of the 159th Air Ambulance Company was asleep, sweating fitfully in the makeshift collection of plywood rectangles that served as their headquarters inside. In the aircraft hangars where the unit's

Blackhawk helicopters were parked, the hangar floor was awash in light. Mechanics and technicians shuffled around the birds that were undergoing routine maintenance. The over-stressed and weary ground crews lumbered around the UH-60A model Blackhawks, replacing components damaged by the furious flying and harsh elements that ground mercilessly at engines, airframes, and electronics. On these helicopters, dedicated to medical evacuation duties, all weapons had been permanently removed. Their defenses were hotrod pilots and five red crosses painted on the birds to mark them as air ambulances. That was supposed to keep the Taliban from shooting at them, but most of the medevac aircrews thought the bright red crosses just gave the enemy a better aiming point.

In the 159th Command Post, a soldier on duty at the operations desk tried to stay awake, his face lit by the glow from multiple computer screens. He stretched and looked around at the room where he stood night watch. He was surrounded by a large table and a dozen chairs used by crews for meetings and briefings. The walls were plastered with maps that were regularly updated with weather and intelligence information. At the back of the high-ceilinged space was the office used by the commanding officer.

The operations soldier slumped back into his chair and noted activity on one of the computer screens. A phone at his elbow rang and he snatched at it while keeping his attention focused on the information scrolling onto the screen. They had a mission and that would be the subject of the phone call. "I see it dropping now!" he said into the phone and reached for a portable radio with his other hand. He pressed the transmit key and sent the alert throughout the compound.

"Medevac, medevac, medevac!" The alert crackled across the airwaves and almost immediately the duty soldier started to get responses as various people and sections checked in to let him know they'd gotten the message.

"MO in route!"

"PC in route!"

"PI in route!"

"CE in route!"

Throughout the tiny compound, doors slammed and the operations soldier could hear boots thumping along the hallways as the crew headed for the operations center. The night duty pilot-in-command (PC), co-pilot (PI), and flight medic (MO) barged through the stampeding bodies and bulled into the ops center. They were greeted with a rapid-fire delivery of vital mission information including grid coordinates, patient numbers, and radio frequencies that they'd need when they got airborne. The flight medic, Staff Sergeant Craig Heathe, snatched a sheet of paper from the duty soldier and scanned the read-out, looking for clues concerning conditions of the patients on the ground among the coded nine-line medevac request. Heathe was a tall, muscular young man, standing straight in his rumpled desert-tan flight suit despite painful back surgery that he'd undergone only a short time past. He ran a hand through a thick shock of quickly graying blonde hair that belied his age. Heathe was only 28, but he'd be running the show tonight.

As usual with a battlefield medevac, time was critical. Patients might well live or die depending on how quickly the helicopter crew could reach the requesting unit. The crew chief grabbed an armful of thick pelican cases containing a computer logbook and drugs. On the way to the door, everyone grabbed M-4 carbines from the ready-rack and slapped loaded magazines into them on the run. The helicopters were unarmed, but everyone flying in them carried personal weapons in case of shoot-downs or other situations which would require them to defend themselves.

The co-pilot grabbed Night Vision Goggles that would be crucial for everyone flying on this night medevac, as well as two heads-up display monocles for the pilots, and then headed out of the building on the run to the 1st up crew's aircraft. The pilot-in-command and the flight medic verified all the mission information and then followed him down the stairs and out of the building. The medevac race was on and Dustoff 2-6 was at the gate.

The Blackhawk was already fueled and waiting on the parking pad as the crew climbed into the aircraft. The crew chief—already in his body armor, survival vest, and helmet— was doing final checks as the pilots vaulted into the cockpit and strapped themselves into their seats. Heathe ran checks on his gear, drug box, and med kit, standing by on the ground with the crew chief. Both of the enlisted men were hooked up to the Blackhawk's communication system and listening for the start-up commands from the pilots, as they checked the ground and the night sky above the Blackhawk for anything that might impact the bird's massive rotors when they began to spin.

They heard the two officers in the cockpit finish the run-up checklist in a few seconds and then the final command that let everyone know they were about to light the engines and engage the rotors: "Clear!"

Flight Medic Heathe and the crew chief both took quick surveys around the intake and exhaust ports of the Blackhawk's engines, and then told the pilots they were clear to spin the blades. As the massive rotors began to whirl, Heathe and the crew chief stood illuminated by the flash of the helicopter's rotating red and green position lights, watching for any fire or other signs of trouble as the engines and rotors spooled up to taxi speed. The noise was deafening, and the aircraft seemed to come alive with power and electronic energy. The pilot advanced the power-control levers on the overhead console to the fly position, and the crew chief scrambled to pull the chocks from around the Blackhawk's wheels. The two men piled into the aircraft like a couple of cowboys doing a saddle-vault onto a familiar mount and strapped themselves in for the take-off roll.

"You guys ready back there?" The pilot was adding power and the aircraft was beginning its roll toward the taxiway.

"Yes, sir. Let's do this." Heathe and the crew chief felt the surge in static electricity as the pilot pulled on his collective and added lift to the rotors.

The aircraft lifted clear of the ground, wobbled a bit as the tail rotor fought the torque imparted by the main blades, and then glided down the taxiway. The main rotor assembly tilted forward under control inputs from the pilots and pulled out the 18,000-pound beast. A soldier on duty along the path waved and smiled as the crew chief leaned out the window and pretended to be paddling a balky canoe. They flew at taxi speed down the active runway that would put them in position for takeoff. Over their headsets, the crew could hear the air traffic controller in Jalabad's tower talking to other aircraft in the area. There was a lot of them this night, including everything from a flight of AH-64D Apaches to a heavy transport from someplace in Europe waiting for landing instructions.

"Skymaster 2-7-2, you're cleared to land runway one three. After landing, proceed abeam taxiway Charlie and hold. Contact ground on frequency 1-1-7..."

The pilot-in-command of Dustoff 2-6 didn't wait for the rest of the transmission. He broke into the frequency and his voice was testy. "Tower, Dustoff 2-6 is an urgent Medevac! Request immediate departure without delay!"

The air controllers put everyone else on hold. They knew what Dustoff was—and they knew what an urgent medevac meant. Somewhere out in the night, a fellow soldier was wounded and needed immediate evacuation from the battlefield. "Copy Dustoff…stand by. Break, break, break. All traffic in vicinity of J'Bad Airfield hold your position. I have a Medevac aircraft outbound to the northwest. Dustoff, you are cleared as requested for immediate departure to the west, early left crosswind. Winds are zero-three-zero at fifteen gusting to twenty, altimeter two-niner-point-eight-two. Report outbound. Have a safe flight."

The pilot-in-command lifted immediately and steered the Blackhawk into the moonless night, pitching the nose forward to gain speed. In the opposite seat, his co-pilot punched coordinates for the pick-up into the GPS system and then reached overhead to flip a switch that turned their lighting system from plain colors to infrared. Dustoff 2-6 would be invisible in the night sky unless the people looking for it were using night vision equipment. It was SOP for night missions. The good guys had NVGs and the bad guys usually did not. The pilots continued to claw for altitude, watching through their NVGs as they flew toward the snow-covered peaks that rose between them and the soldiers somewhere on the other side, waiting for help.

In the back of Dustoff 2-6, Staff Sergeant Craig did what he could to prepare for a mission that was a mystery, and would remain that way until they arrived over the battlefield. He mentally reviewed all his training, all the possible protocols and interventions he might have to perform on this op.

It was probably going to be a hoist given the terrain in the area where the wounded were waiting, and he hated doing hoist missions at night. Getting a wounded soldier off the ground and into the medevac aircraft by hoist meant he would have to climb onto a hook dangling outside a machine that always seemed to be thrashing itself to pieces as the pilots fought to hold a steady hover. *How many more of these will I have to do*, he wondered. *How many more can I do?*

As many as I need to do, he reassured himself as he stared down into the darkness at the rugged terrain flowing below the Blackhawk, *because no matter how scared I am, there's a wounded guy on the ground that's twice as scared. And I'm all he's got.*

The flight seemed to take forever and it was all boring routine until the crew chief made his move toward the back of the cabin. The pilots had contact with the requesting unit on the ground and it was time for the show to start. "We're two minutes out," the pilot said over the intercom and Heathe unbuckled to begin final checks. He made sure the crew chief's monkey strap that linked to the back of his survival vest and kept him from falling out of the aircraft was secure. If they caught a gust of unexpected wind or had to maneuver hard to avoid ground fire, that strap was all the crew chief had to keep him connected with the aircraft. The crew chief returned the favor by checking Heathe's gear and then reported they were set for the pick-up.

"Buddy checks complete."

"Roger," the co-pilot said. "We're slowing up now—got them in sight."

The crew chief announced that he was opening the cargo door and then pulled the right side door back to keep it from slamming shut when Heathe was suspended outside on the hoist. He reached for the hoist's hand control and then sat on the vibrating metal floor with his legs dangling in the night air. The hoist swung out into position for a descent and Heathe straddled a three-prong hook called a jungle penetrator or JP that he would ride to the ground, carrying a collapsible litter that looked like a big olive-drab Tootsie Roll covered with straps to secure a patient during the lift.

Perched on the JP and exposed to the cool night air, Heathe sat motionless as the slipstream blasted his face. He could see nothing on the ground as the Blackhawk slowed. The nose pitched up like a motorcycle doing a wheelie as the pilots bled off airspeed. Heathe felt the hoist line swinging toward the tail rotor as the crew chief began to drop him into the night. He could see the ground now and had a panoramic view of the Kunar Valley.

The crew chief had the same view, but he was focused on getting his flight medic safely on the ground—pressing the descent button on his hand control, he kept a hand encased in a thick welder's glove on the JP cable, feeling for any snags or snarls. They were over the proposed pick-up site now, and the pilots pulled Dustoff 2-6 into a hover, causing the entire aircraft to shudder as the men in the cockpit fought to hold it steady.

With his feet outstretched and body leaned back to minimize spinning or oscillations, Heathe dropped into the shadows while the crew chief reported his progress to the pilots.

"Hold hover...three, two, one...medic is on the ground."

In the aircraft cockpit over Heathe's head, the pilot-in-command was fighting the night winds that were blowing down across the valley from the high ground and trying to maintain a point of view that would help him hold a hover in position over the pick-up site. He scanned the starry sky in a steady pattern through his NVGs, looking for visual cues that would help him keep the aircraft in exactly the same spot while the medic on the surface got his patients evaluated and hooked up for the lift. With Heathe safely on the ground, the crew chief reeled the hoist line back up to keep it from blowing into a tree or snagging some other vertical obstruction while they waited for Heathe to signal he was ready to send up the patients.

✍

On the mountain, Heathe was reassuring the soldiers that their wounded were in good hands. "Hey, don't worry," he told the circle of grunts helping him with the patients. "I'm gonna get these guys out of here." They loaded the first wounded man on the collapsible stretcher and Heathe grabbed a nearby soldier to assist him with the lift. It all worked better if one of the grunts controlled the length of rope—called a tag line—to keep the stretcher and the medic from spinning on the way up to the aircraft. "Just keep a little tension on the line," Heathe told the soldier, "so we don't spin. The hoist will do the rest."

Heathe clipped into the cable ring, checked on the wounded man, and signaled for the crew chief to start lifting. He talked calmly to the wounded soldier as they rode the hoist and was happy to see the man's relieved sighs in response. He was safe now, as good as out of it, and that was the best medicine in a situation like this. As they disappeared into the night sky, the wounded man's buddies shouted reassurances to Bradbury.

"You're gonna make it, bro!"

"Don't worry about us out here; don't worry about anything."

"Take care of yourself. We'll see you soon, Brian."

Heathe and Bradbury were rising steadily toward the hovering Blackhawk as the crew chief reported their progress to the pilots. "Hover looks good. Medic and patient are thirty feet below the cabin, twenty feet...wait!" There was a loud snap, sharp and distinct despite the roar of the engines and the chop of the rotors. It sounded like a bullwhip cracking and it echoed through the helicopter's cabin.

"I lost him!" The crew chief leaned out of the aircraft holding onto a short length of frayed steel hoist cable, staring into the dark below his perch. "CRAIG!" he screamed as Heathe and the wounded man plummeted to the ground a hundred feet below the Blackhawk. The soldiers on the ground scattered when they heard the snap of the hoist line and now they were all rushing toward the two limp forms lying silently on the rocks. The Taliban had nothing to do with it—but they were now going to have to deal with two other fallen heroes.

CHAPTER 2: CAV COUNTRY

**Heroes may not be braver than anyone else.
They're just braver 5 minutes longer.**

—Ronald Reagan

FOB Shank, Afghanistan
14 January 2011

MY DAY HAD FINALLY COME. I stood out in front of the oversized doghouse that served as Command Post for Forward Operating Base Shank and wondered at what I was feeling. I hated this place—but I was going to miss it. My commander had ordered me to move to Jalalabad for the upcoming fighting season.

Squinting against the sandy wind, I stared up at the place that had been my home for too long in Afghanistan. The CP had dark brown adobe walls and its unfinished roof was crowded with antenna arrays. It looked like the home of some squatter family that won the lottery and spent the money on a bunch of satellite TV receivers. On one side of the building was a little jerry-rigged porch area covered in camouflage netting. That porch connected the CP to the aid station next door where the ground medics and flight doctors hung out. The porch had been a special project for the 1st Platoon, Forward Support Medical Team, what everyone called the FSMT, and we were proud of it.

My platoon, flying the medevac helicopters out of FOB Shank, was deployed up here early, ahead of the full Task Force that eventually arrived to patrol this turbulent area of

Afghanistan. While we waited, I had made some friends in the outgoing unit and from among the locals in the villages surrounding the base. Through a series of mostly legal transactions, I managed to scrounge air conditioners, building materials, power tools, and nearly everything else needed to convert the porch into a fairly well-appointed enclosed lounge for my platoon—a favorite place to hang out between missions. We even built a fake broom closet that held the only entrance. When people came to the lounge looking for 1st Platoon soldiers to handle various irritating jobs, we often just ran to the broom closet and disappeared into our bat cave which kept us hidden until the irritating people found someone else for their irritating little jobs. We flew Dustoff missions—and that was hard enough work without additional fatigue details.

I was gonna miss this place.

Fortunately, my platoon leader and platoon sergeant turned a blind eye to my nest-building penchant; even on the day I had a 40-foot steel shipping container suspended precariously over their office on a rusty construction crane. It was just as well they walked away from the site as a daredevil Afghan rode the box into place while I wrestled to control its descent with a thin length of ratty rope. We managed to land the container right on the mark between our area and the adjacent CP of the Pathfinders that were the host unit at FOB Shank. The big shipping box served as our secret stash where we kept goodies and supplies for our guys stuck out in the hinterlands at FOB Ghazni, an extremely remote outpost to the south occupied by a very under-provisioned Polish Army unit. One could only eat Polish sausage and instant potatoes for so long. We all rotated through stints at FOB Ghazni, but we usually had lickies, chewies, and other supplies we needed from the stock maintained in our stash at Shank.

Our unit was a red-headed step-child among others regularly attached to Task Forces in the area. They had short supply pipelines while ours was lengthy and convoluted. I saw that as more like a challenge than a problem. Like an Army Robin Hood, I stole from the rich to supply the poor—namely, the poor 1st Platoon of the FSMT. I quickly discovered that it was easier and more efficient to just do what needed to be done rather than go through the long-winded, bureaucratic process of asking permission. I was a Warrant Officer; it was my job to find solutions to problems, not inundate the boss man with gripes and complaints.

But I was now set to see FOB Shank and all my comfortable additions disappear in a rearview mirror. Orders arrived sending me to the 4th Platoon FSMT, located at Jalalabad—home to serious spooks and special operators who worked close to the Pakistan border. J'bad was not a prime posting, but orders were orders.

I was scheduled for transfer on a flight that never arrived, so it appeared that I was on my own hook to get myself and my gear to Jalalabad. Our Task Force Operations Officer, Captain Cattanach, was in his office when I appeared wondering how I might get the move accomplished. He had been my platoon leader the previous year in Iraq. He was a tall, confident West Pointer who knew his way around official roadblocks.

He smiled at me and pointed toward the airfield. "Sabby, there is an aircraft out there now. You're not manifested on it, but..."

"...if I hurry, I can catch it," I said, finishing his sentence. He wished me good luck as I shook his hand and then bolted out the door. My Platoon Sergeant, Sergeant First Class

Mike Walker, was cursing at me to get a move on. I ran up to him sitting in a four-wheel John Deere gator. I said good-bye to the rest of the guys and jammed my gear into the vehicle. I gave my best friend CW2 Tom Streit a bear-hug and hopped in as we peeled away, my face coated with the powdered sugar-like sand. The only thing I noticed during the break-neck race to the airstrip was a huge white aerostat blimp hanging over the desert like a Nerf ball. It was packed with instruments that monitored the enemy and sent us information that made flying just a touch easier for flight crews operating out of FOB Shank.

There was a small civilian transport aircraft on the ramp being pre-flighted by a couple of guys in shorts and t-shirts. They had no other passengers and plenty of room, so I hopped in with just my hand luggage, feeling like Indiana Jones escaping from some horrible predicament. The pilots climbed in after me, closed the loading ramp, and fired up the engines. In a few minutes, we were airborne and turning in the direction of J'bad. My Platoon Sergeant promised to send my other gear along on another flight, so there was not much to ponder beyond what might be waiting for me with the 4th Platoon. Jalalabad was surrounded by steep mountains, and that would make for some interesting flight challenges at the controls of a Blackhawk.

We landed after dark, but I managed to find a phone and the number of the 4th Platoon CP. Sergeant Johnny Reyes arrived shortly after I hung up with a vehicle to take me and my gear to the unit. He was an old pal from other assignments, and he ignored the handshake to hoist me with another bear-hug. It was a good start. At least someone at my new outfit was glad to see me.

"What's cracking, Cracker?" Reyes swung me into his vehicle and announced that my boxes containing the rest of my gear had arrived on another flight.

"You old saltwater wetback—it's good to see you again." Reyes grabbed my flight gear bag and cranked the engine. He swung the wheel and we roared down the road past concrete barriers and makeshift wooden buildings on our way to the CP. Reyes was a stout, muscular operations soldier from Guam, and smarter than almost everyone he met. He ran a gaggle of radio operators who spent most of their time locked onto computer screens, where they monitored medevac missions that Reyes said were dropping on the unit like an avalanche as combat action around Jalalabad gained intensity. Reyes' techies also kept the unit's radios, equipment, and personal weapons ready for instant action. When it came down to basics, his guys handled everything that didn't directly involve flying or medical matters. Reyes knew how important they were to the overall mission and he conducted both himself and his squad with appropriate gravitas. Johnny Reyes was a no-nonsense NCO, and even the laid-back pilots didn't mess with him or his men. I'd always secretly thought Reyes was some sort of island voodoo practitioner. Somewhere out there in the Pacific near the Marianas Islands, Sgt. Reyes had likely fed a few enemies to the fishes. He was a tough hombre during the high-altitude training we went through in Colorado prior to deployment, and I'd spent some time with him and his men during that evolution.

One thing was obvious as we neared the 4th Platoon CP. Jalalabad was located well below the altitude I was used to from my time at FOB Shank. It was nearly 5,000 feet lower, which made breathing easier, and told me flying down in the valleys would be easier on aircraft and crews. Of course, we'd probably find ourselves flying up into the mountains that surrounded the base, but I had learned to take the good stuff in stride and worry about the bad stuff when it happened. Worrying about it beforehand was a recipe for migraines.

Those mountains were visible on the moonlit horizon, and staring up at them made me feel small and insignificant. How would I make out in an aircraft chopping through the thin air up there on the way to pick up wounded men? As Reyes wheeled into the base proper, we saw Afghan soldiers with AK-47s patrolling the area. I got a chill down my spine. Something here was different; I just couldn't put my finger on it. Something less than good.

I got some sleep and then made my rounds to meet the 4th Platoon people that were my new coworkers. There were a couple of days spent filling out paperwork, listening to briefings, and getting a feel for how the unit operated. Much of settling into a new outfit is knowing who the power players are and how they operate. 4th Platoon was a very tight outfit, and all of them were fully aware of the importance of J'bad to the war effort. Among Army aviators, it wasn't so much a choice assignment as it was the place to be. J'bad was where the action happened quickly and regularly: the site of the craziest, hairiest missions available to flight crews. Gun pilots routinely vied for a slot here in order to get more trigger time. The base had absorbed the city's airport, and it had a long rep as an action hub. It was where Osama Bin Laden first entered Afghanistan and where he departed as a bullet-riddled corpse after the SEALs whacked him across the border in Pakistan.

Everywhere you looked there were silent, steely-eyed types that the smart survivor tried very hard not to challenge or irritate in any fashion. Jalalabad was bristling with operators and somehow the flight crews from 4th Platoon Dustoff had enough swagger and panache to fit right in with them.

Our CP was unique. It resembled a frontier ranch house and even featured a cow bell that was used to call the hands to chow. I was happy to note that the cabin had a porch, and the centerpiece of that structure was a huge brick oven with a side grill perfect for barbecues. The old hands in 4th Platoon told me sometimes the Green Berets brought steaks, chicken, or other meat and enjoyed a cookout with us. Those occasions were a treat.

The barbecue porch abutted J'bad's taxiway and led to an expanse of concrete that doubled as parking space for three Blackhawks and several AH-64D Apache attack helicopters which belonged to the 6-6 Air Cavalry Task Force to which we were assigned. Across the way were OH-58D Scout helicopters and CH-47F Chinooks, the Army's heavy lifters. The Cav soldiers had adopted the Dustoff aviators and even painted a huge red and white "Cavalry Dustoff" flag on the front steps leading to our CP. I soon drank the Kool Aid and joined the Cav—it was a great unit to be a part of.

On one side of our headquarters at J'bad was a row of metal shipping containers with deteriorating decks that showed their age, but gave us a grand view of the whole area when we climbed up to take a look at the surrounding terrain. The CP area had been overrun with large desert lizards that crawled everywhere out of the shade to bask in the hot sun and disappeared to their lairs at dark. Inside our operations center, one entire wall was lined with weapons and equipment. There were also tables, chairs and several homemade desks, fronting a couple of private offices. In the back was a room with cubbyholes that stored flight gear for the crews.

The most welcome feature amid all the standard furniture was a small phone booth with a door that provided privacy for phone calls to the States. Soldiers in Dustoff were restricted to the CP or their rooms, but they were permitted to use their individual credit cards for personal phone calls to families or friends back home. It was a greatly appreciated luxury.

There was a little snack-eating area, with a fridge covered in stickers from other units that had been there before us, that connected 4th Platoon's area to the CP of the air-cavalry Apache drivers. I stayed away from that at first. I hadn't had much experience with Army Apaches back at FOB Shank. There were many times on missions when we had the Polish pilots in Russian-built Mi-24 Hind gunships flying cover for us. I'd never hung out with scout or attack pilots. You flew your aircraft, but you became your mission. Over the years in the U.S. Army, Apache pilots and Blackhawk flight crews had developed a good-natured rivalry that developed into a degree of mutual toleration.

For instance, there is often an unofficial question hidden in the Blackhawk's pilot's *Study Guide of Emergency Procedures* that asks: How do you get a one-armed Apache pilot out of a tree? Flip the card over and the answer is: Wave to him. But I tried to keep the rivalry subdued and avoid clashes between fellow aviators. I was at J'bad with the 4th Platoon of the FSMT to learn and then fly to the best of my ability, so I kept my mouth shut and listened as my new assignment began. For me, keeping my mouth shut has sometimes proved challenging.

J'bad itself was a wild, remote border city, nestled in the foothills of the infamous Tora Bora Mountains just 15 minutes flying time from Pakistan. A massive gap in the mountains to the north marked the entry to the Kunar Valley.

The base was only about 1,800 feet above mean sea level, but the surrounding mountains featured peaks that rose to more than 14,000 feet. I wouldn't be up there long enough to get cold, so I stowed my winter flight clothing and then moved in to a hovel marked Pilots' Penthouse with the rest of the Blackhawk drivers from the 4th Platoon.

By dawn on my second day at J'bad, I was on the flight schedule. The platoon worked a cycle to man three Black-hawks ready on call as required. It was called lining up "in the chute." One crew would be first-up in the chute with sec-ond-up resting on standby and third-up ready to go if things got particularly hairy. Usually, the first-up crew would launch on any medevac mission that came down to us. If we were lucky, we would be chased, or escorted, by a UH-60L Blackhawk that carried door gunners. If none of them were available, we would chase ourselves or rely on an Apache or OH-58D Kiowa scout bird if they were available. Since we carried no offensive weapons, any armed escort was appre-ciated. Landing Zones and pick-up sites for medevacs around J'bad tended to be hot properties. If we managed to get ourselves shot down on a mission and survived the crash, we could scramble for what was called a "spur ride" on an Apache or a Kiowa. Neither of those aircraft had passenger compartments, so we were expected to just latch onto some-thing on the fuselage and hang on until the escort flew us to safety. I'd never done a spur ride—and that was fine by me.

I was up hours early on my first duty day with 4th Pla-toon, watching the flight crews for signs of nervousness or trepidation. There was no sign that anyone expected any-thing out of the ordinary. We started the helicopters, checked the radios, did function-checks on the hoists, and then took turns going back for breakfast. In Iraq, casualties were fre-quently gathered into aircraft that had landed on the nice, flat

ground. Here in eastern Afghanistan, the mountainous terrain meant that landing was often not an option. Instead, a
medic goes down on the hoist, performs any first aid or rescue that's needed, and then is hoisted back up into the aircraft with the patient. This hair-raising operation meant that
not only did the pilot have to keep the aircraft level, but also
that there was a live person out there going up and down on
that hoist. Everyone had to know what was going on in the
aircraft, both front and back. But this morning it was all familiar routine and no one seemed overly concerned as they
scanned the morning briefs. Maybe this was not going to be
as bad as advertised.

After chow in the CP which was just a short sprint away
from the aircraft parking area, I fiddled around the flight line
thinking about the Dustoff mission. A wounded soldier in
Afghanistan had a 92 percent chance of survival—and that
was due to us. We normally got a wounded soldier to a surgeon in an hour or less, which meant they would likely survive. In the hands of an experienced flight crew, a
Blackhawk could be airborne in about ten minutes from the
time the alert call arrived. Most medevac crews beat that
time—and were flying in half the time or less. It was a matter
of pride and professionalism. We cut corners when necessary, but we got up and gone in short order when lives were
on the line.

As the new guy in 4th Platoon, I was assigned as co-pilot
to my platoon leader while he checked me out on the area of
responsibility. Captain Drew Wilson was a tall, pasty-faced
redhead that I knew from previous assignments. His father
was an Air Force F-15 fighter pilot and he'd inherited some
of his Dad's fighter-jock cockiness. Drew and I had been together through Survival, Evasion, Resistance, and Escape
training, what the military calls SERE. He was a solid Army

aviator, but his commission was in the Medical Service Corps, so he was already destined for Dustoff Blackhawks from the moment he got accepted into flight school. I had to wait for months after basic qualification before I found out what the Army wanted me to fly. While I was waiting, I ran into Drew in a store and he was all full of himself about that day's flying. "Oh yeah," he said in a voice loud enough to be heard by every shopper in the store. "I found my hover button today!"

There was an instructor pilot standing next to me in the check-out line. He elbowed me and whispered, "And I'm betting he loses it tomorrow." There was no sense in bursting Drew Wilson's bubble right then. Like a lot of other budding Army helicopter pilots I was still struggling to find my own hover button.

Drew and I parted company at Fort Drum, New York. He went to Dustoff and I got sent to the Air Assault battalion where my job was to deliver soldiers into combat aboard Blackhawks so they could kill people and break their stuff. We were all training for eventual deployment to Iraq, which was the campaign *du jour* in the ongoing war on terrorism. Drew had had a tough year in Iraq, and when we met again at J'bad, he seemed to have mellowed a bit. He still had a taste of the old fighter-jock panache but he was more sober and subdued flying as a pilot-in-command.

On our first flight through the AO, I was simply along for the ride as a new guy getting a feel for the territory. We lifted off with a flight crew consisting of people I would get to know intimately over the days and weeks to come. Sergeant Phillip Vaughn flew as crew chief. He was a happy-go-lucky Soldier with a penchant for practical jokes. Sergeant Julia Bringloe was our Flight Medic. She seemed to be a calm and capable pro who had been a ground medic before she transferred to Dustoff. I got the impression from watching her work and listening to her terse talk over the intercom that she was just what the other crews said she was: tough as nails.

Although this was my first experience with Bringloe as regular crew, I'd flown briefly with her at Fort Drum, New York when we were spooling up for deployment. She was new to the outfit and flew with us in an effort to gain experience. If she was tentative back then getting a feel for flying and working with a crew, she was dialed in tightly now by her experience with 4th Platoon. She was comfortable in the air and in her other duties, and it was hard to tell she'd only been flying Dustoff for a year or so, having just recently gotten her first combat hoist.

That calm, professional demeanor was important for the kind of work we did as medevac support for troops in contact. The practiced, well-choreographed communication and drills among medevac crews was critical to survival—for patients and for the helicopter crew. The pilots' view on missions was limited to what they could see forward and in a limited area out the sides of the cockpit. When we needed to know what was happening beyond that—and that's most of the time after we arrived at the pick-up site—the crew chiefs and flight medics in the back served as our eyes. They talked to us all the time, providing a word picture of what was going on around us as we flew. Many of the phrases we used were standardized and mandatory, so there was little chance for misunderstanding or misinterpretation.

The key was to be specific and unemotional in communications within the aircraft. It wasn't helpful to hear something like "Oh, no!" or some expletive when something went wrong in flight. What we needed up in the cockpit, and what crew members were trained to communicate when they spot a problem, is specific information on what that problem was so we could do something useful to solve it. Anything short of that just left everyone to stress out and fire questions over the ICS. That took time, and in an emergency time is crucial to survival. Pilots learn to trust the crew's judgment. A good pilot, trusting a good crew chief or flight medic, often returns from a near disaster with nothing more to show for it than a good war story. In the Dustoff business where lives are always on the line, one of the hardest things for flight crews to do is to suppress their emotions and stay focused on flying and saving lives.

Just before lunch, a radio call from Sgt. Reyes brought me and the rest of my crew to the CP. There was no indication of panic, but all of us knew a routine summons like this could rapidly morph into an urgent mission. Five months of flying medevacs in Afghanistan had taught us to be prepared for the unexpected to happen anytime. It could be nothing or it could be one of the three basic types of missions we were called on to fly. The ground guys would call higher, and they would relay to us what was up. Our missions were classified according to the problem being experienced by the unit calling for a medevac.

Routine was the lowest priority. That could be anything from a case of dehydration to a non-life threatening medical situation like a dental problem. Next up on the scale was a Priority Medevac, which usually involved something like a non-life threatening gunshot or shrapnel wound. It might also involve a broken bone or something else if it didn't threaten the patient's life or hinder the unit's movement. The big deal for us was an Urgent Medevac request. When those came in, the soldiers on the ground had determined that there was a high probability that a wounded soldier might die, lose a limb or their eyesight if we didn't get them off the battle-field and back to medical treatment as soon as possible.

Like every other pilot or flight crewmember flying Dustoff, I'd spent a good deal of time thinking about battle-field evacuation and the chain of medical care a modern soldier receives after we pick him up out of the fight. In our situation flying in Afghanistan, the drill involved bringing the wounded man back to Jalalabad where he'd be stabilized. Then, our Headquarters Platoon would send another aircraft to pick him up for transport back to the hospital at Bagram, where he would get more advanced treatment or emergency surgery. The most critical patients were then transported by Air Force C-17s to Germany, where their combat deployment usually ended. It saved a lot of lives that might otherwise be lost, but it was a double-edged sword and all of us knew that. A lot more wounded soldiers lived because of the speed of medevac aircraft, but many of them, horribly torn up by IEDs or other modern weapons, faced long, difficult, and painful rehabilitation. It was a chain of pain and it never seemed to end, but the words on our unit patch said *To Save a Life* and there's a lot of motivation in that.

As we entered the ops area, we heard scratchy conversations on a couple of different radios, punctuated by the tell-tale beeps of transmissions on secure frequencies that were designed to foil enemy monitoring. Johnny Reyes pointed at one of his computer screens and let us know why we were summoned. "Falcon Med Ops just called and said you've got a routine dropping." The mission brief told us the patient was at a small FOB to the east of us and just a few miles from the Pakistan border. The patient was in no immediate danger, suffering from a stomach bug that was making him too sick to patrol. Ops decided he could wait for a while and we would hang around to see if any other requests came in that would make our trip more efficient and economical. At least that was the theory, and it was understandable from the military point of view—but it had drawbacks.

Jumping on every routine mission immediately was hard on crews and often forced the command to swap them out early to avoid accidents caused by crew fatigue. The last thing any of us wanted was to be exhausted from a long day of flying when an urgent medevac request came along in the wee hours of a morning. Missions kept coming in and they had to be flown somehow by somebody. Unfortunately, pilots can't just pull a Blackhawk over to the side of the road for a little rest when they get tired. I've spent ten hours in an aircraft and I didn't enjoy it. You just have to keep reminding yourself that it's easier for you than it is for the guy in a fox-hole on the ground.

As co-pilot—or Peter Pilot—on the crew I wanted to get on with the mission and just go get the guy. We could fly out there, pick him up, and bring him back to J'bad, which would save all of us from drilling holes in the sky on a multiple pick-up mission. Waiting around for another mission that we could combine with the first one was irritating. Fatigue sets in quickly when you're locked in the cockpit of a big vibrating sauna like the Blackhawk. Your concentration dwindles and drifts after long periods on the flight controls being shaken by the airframe and battered by the engine noise. The Blackhawk is one of the noisiest helicopters in the Army inventory. While our helmets cancel some of the roar, constant radio chatter can batter your brain to mush on a long mission.

At this point, as we hung around ops waiting for another mission, things got interesting. "Sir, we got another one up in the Kunar...grid to follow." Reyes pointed at one of his computer screens.

"Where is it?" Wilson, our pilot-in-command, looked up from the map he was studying.

"It's up north a bit, right on the border," Reyes said. He pointed out a small hill on the map that looked like it was very close to Pakistan.

"That's pretty close. Is it a routine?"

"Yep; they're saying it's nothing serious."

Wilson thought it over for a minute and made his decision. "OK. Tell Falcon Med Ops we'll combine them and launch on both."

We were about to go flying at last. I squeezed between Wilson and Reyes, reaching for my M-4 and headed for the door. Our crew chief SGT Vaughn followed me, spooning ice cream from the bowl he'd just gotten. Our flight medic SGT Bringloe stayed with Wilson, conferring with Captain Ledlow, our unit Flight Surgeon, who would fly with us on the mission.

I was at the Blackhawk doing a walk-around when they arrived at the aircraft. We had drawn a winner for this mission. The helicopter was a UH-60A+ that featured several improvements over the older, lighter A models introduced in the 1970s. The biggest upgrade on the alpha plus were the more powerful engines which gave the Blackhawk lots of lift at higher altitudes.

While the other crew got their equipment sorted out, I donned my flight gear and took a good look at the helicopter. It was a stout ride despite the chips and fading on the mottled paint job that came from long service and the effects of Afghanistan's merciless sunlight. Still, it was a beautiful beast to me: A dark green, dolphin-shaped world-beater with four large black main rotor blades hanging from the top like diving boards straining under their own weight. It was a good day to fly a Blackhawk. The alpha plus was the ultimate flying machine, capable of any conceivable mission, and the fastest Blackhawk in the world. I cracked open the cockpit door, climbed in, and started running through the start-up checklist.

We were off the ground quickly after everyone else was aboard and settled. Wilson let me do the flying and I held it back a bit for the crew of the slower UH-60L, call-sign "Chill," which was our escort on the mission. I'm no stick pig, but I did appreciate having the controls to myself. Below us was the standard Afghanistan topography and there was a lot of it to view as I held our airspeed at about 120 knots indicated. It's a lonesome place to see from altitude, a dappled mixture of desert expanses interspersed with squares of poorly irrigated green that marked local farms. In between these patches were strings of rolling hills that looked like anthills. Mostly because it's more fun to maneuver than it is to fly in a straight line, I swung the Blackhawk around these features, being gentle with the control inputs but getting a good look at everything unrolling below us. It was early in the morning and the air was smooth. The sun had yet to heat the earth sufficiently to bring on the turbulence caused by rising hot air.

Reaching down on the side of my seat with my left hand, I set the collective by tightening the friction collar that would hold it in place at my selected setting of about 70 percent torque or power. Then I nudged the cyclic control forward to lower the nose and gain some airspeed. When it was where I wanted it, I released the trim button and took my hands off the controls. The bird was flying itself now, and it would

hold my selected profile until I changed the settings or it re-
acted to some other influence like a strong gust of wind. It
was beautiful flying—the kind of thing that kept me happy
in the cockpit and wanting more. "They pay me to do this,"
I said, shaking my head a little in disbelief.

It was easy to drift in a situation like this, easy to get lost
in the experience and forget the mission. A lot of bad things
can happen in a helicopter if the pilot is lost in reverie, so I
tightened my focus, adjusted my seat downward, and got a
little less comfortable behind the side armor that Vaughn had
adjusted for me while he was finishing his bowl of ice cream.
I was behind the power curve this morning, missing some of
the little common tasks that should be routine. It's at times
like these that a pilot can get caught by surprise by unexpected events and be just a little slow in responding. Slow in
responding is high on the list of bad things for a helicopter
pilot to be.

We were about two minutes out from our destination
when we saw a civilian helicopter pass on our left side in the
opposite direction. When we made contact with the aircraft,
we learned that it was a contractor bird and that they had our
patient aboard. My PC Wilson was unhappy that we were
not notified that the patient had hitchhiked a ride with the
civilians. We'd flown a long way for nothing, but I wasn't
upset. I got some good stick time and a tour of our eastern
battlespace. We were swinging around to head back to J'bad
when our pleasant flight was rudely interrupted.

"Dustoff 7-3...Dustoff 7-3, this is Ops, how do you
hear?" It was Johnny Reyes calling on our unit medevac frequency.

"Ops this is 7-3...go," Wilson responded.

"Dustoff 7-3, we have an urgent nine-line at FOB Gamberi. It's multiple wounded."

"You guys hear that?" I radioed to our escort Blackhawk to be sure they monitored the call. They heard and I got back on the controls, pushing for more airspeed. The plus-model roared away under all the power I could get out of the engines and the heavier escort bird began to fall behind. They could catch up with us later. Right now, urgent meant we were needed in a hurry. Details began to come in over the radio from J'bad.

A suicide bomber had detonated his body at FOB Gamberi, and there were a bunch of wounded men requiring evacuation. We didn't know much more than that at first. The LZ was unknown and they were finding additional wounded, so there was no good count on how many we would be expected to haul. It was somewhat less than ideal but that's the way it happens sometimes.

As we approached the FOB, I spotted the aerostat blimp marking Gamberi shining through the haze and swung the aircraft in that direction. Wilson was on the radio trying to raise someone on the ground and having no luck. We could see the chaos with people running in all directions as we passed over the base. Without guidance from someone on the ground, it was hard to tell where we were needed. Our crew chief Vaughn solved that problem.

"Right rear has the building in sight," Vaughn called over the ICS. I looked over my shoulder to see a structure sitting in a field of gravel that had been heavily damaged by an explosion. Windows and doors were lying on the ground amid rubble and twisted metal that fanned out like confetti on every side of the building. Only the outer walls looked intact, but they were blackened with powder residue.

As we turned looking for a space with room enough to land, I saw vehicles with Red Crescents painted on them parked near the structure. We wouldn't know anything else until we landed. I told the crew that I planned to put the Blackhawk down on a nearby road and to be alert for secondary detonations, which was always a threat after an IED detonation. The bad guys knew helicopters would be called, and they often set up more explosives to damage or destroy other aircraft. There wasn't much I could do about that except pray, so I did that and dropped the aircraft toward the ground.

Vaughn was out of the aircraft the moment we settled and he surveyed the area. "I don't see the patients," he said. "Just a bunch of ANA dudes." The Afghan National Army soldiers didn't look like they knew what was happening either, but someone had a grip on the situation. The radio crackled with a message. "Dustoff aircraft, we have an LZ marked with a VS-17 panel. How copy?" So, someone wanted us to get airborne and look for a large orange plastic sheet that would tell us where the wounded were being assembled. It was a standard marking for helicopters and easy to see if you're flying over a grassy field or forested area. Out in the desert, flying at altitude, a VS-17 just looks like all the rest of the trash that has accumulated over the last few thousand years.

"Get in!" Wilson said to bring Vaughn back inside the aircraft. "I think I know where they are."

"You have the controls," I said, taking my hands off the cyclic and collective and my feet off the pedals.

"I have the controls," Wilson said, waiting for Vaughn to report that he was back inside the Blackhawk. He lifted us quickly, swinging the aircraft to the right. He had his eyes on something in the distance that I couldn't see from my position. As we flew low over the area, I spotted a narrow gravel-covered walled-in courtyard. The courtyard ran north-south and it was surrounded by vehicles. There was an orange square VS-17 flapping in our rotor-wash as we flew over the place. Wilson decided he would put the aircraft down as close as possible, and I radioed the escort Blackhawk to follow us in for some gun cover or to pick up extra casualties if we got a full load. They copied the transmission and told us they would land behind us wherever they could find space. As Wilson dove us toward the objective, we could see dozens of wounded scattered all over the yard, covered in blood with tattered remnants of clothing and equipment scattered everywhere.

It was a tight fit for a landing. Antennae on the surrounding vehicles were only about 15 feet from our rotor disk on either side of the aircraft but Wilson didn't seem rattled. "This isn't an LZ," he said as he concentrated on maneuvering the bird through ground effect. "This is the motor pool."

"The aid station must be that shack up ahead," I said, keeping my eyes on a structure at one end of the parking lot where I could see people trying to treat casualties. Everyone in the back was focused on getting us down in the tight area and keeping a sharp eye out for anything that might obstruct the tail rotor.

"Continue forward...five, four, three, two, one...clear down right." Vaughn was helping us from his position in the right rear of the aircraft.

"Clear down left." Bringloe said from her position on the other side. We touched down with a bounce and the cabin doors flew open for litter teams that were running toward us carrying wounded. And there were a lot of wounded that day at FOB Gamberi.

"Look at them all!" I said. Getting all these people out was going to require help from the escort aircraft on the ground behind us. "Vaughn, you better get back to Chill," I transmitted sending him back to talk to the escort, "and have them pull seats."

"Already on it, Sir!" Vaughn was dashing back toward our escort aircraft carrying a load of medical gear they'd need, now that they were serving as a second Dustoff. Flight Medic Bringloe and Flight Surgeon Captain Ledlow were on the ground shouting at each other over the engine noise, assessing the wounded, and getting them organized for evacuation with efficient speed. Ledlow would fly with our escort since they didn't carry a medic, and all of the wounded would need care during the evacuation flight. Most of the wounded were in really rough shape as the guys on the ground crammed them into both of our mission aircraft.

There were screams in the cabin behind my seat and I craned around to see a heavyset civilian in a khaki shirt grabbing at his legs. A wounded soldier was unceremoniously laid next to him. The wounded soldier was spiked with IV tubes and blood flowed from his nose down onto his chest. He was unconscious and being attended by Bringloe. Every patient was oozing blood from multiple holes, filled with rocks, metal, and pieces of the suicide bomber. She looked up to see two other patients headed our way and took a quick look to determine how bad they were hurt. She decided they were better stabilized on the ground and that we could pick them up on a return trip.

We had a full load of people who really needed to get to medical help in a hurry. Vaughn jumped in and shouted "Go, go!" Wilson pulled pitch and we rocketed up over the landing zone. As we clawed for altitude I called Chill who was flying the escort bird.

"Chill, we can't wait. See you back at J'bad."

"Roger, Dustoff," he replied. "We're right behind you."

While Wilson poured power to the aircraft and put us on a direct course for J'bad, I got busy on the radios. As we came in sight of the base, I alerted the crew in the back to prepare for landing and then got ops and gave them our ETA. They were ready for us.

"Roger, Sir," said Johnny Reyes. He was on top of the situation as usual and his voice was calm. "We've got the Forward Surgical Team ready on the ramp. Be advised Gamberi is now declaring a MASCAL. They've got over forty wounded. How copy?" It was clearly worse than the evidence we saw on the first trip, a Mass Casualty event. We'd be going back to FOB Gamberi in a hurry once we got this first load turned over to the ground medics. I switched to the air traffic control frequency and let J'bad tower know we'd need priority clearance to land both Blackhawks.

"JAF tower, Dustoff 7-3 is a flight of two we're five to the west inbound with urgent medevacs."

"Roger, Dustoff. Will you or chase be refueling?"

"Negative. Both aircraft will depart immediately for more patients after landing." In a situation like this one, you go with the fuel you've got assuming you can make the flight without running dry.

It was a bad day for all concerned and I suddenly missed the relatively calmer duty at FOB Shank as we landed and rolled toward the ambulances waiting on the ramp. Waiting for us were about 20 people of every rank in various stages of dress, standing by to help carry patients off the aircraft. They knew we needed to be unloaded and gone as quickly as possible. Behind me in the cabin, I could see Bringloe straddling one of the patients still on a stretcher, pumping furiously on the man's chest as she tried to keep him alive. She stayed with the man, performing CPR along the way as a litter party carried them both to an ambulance. He was critical, so she jumped into the ambulance with him which meant we would have to fly the next load minus our Flight Medic. I tried to get my buddy Chief Warrant Officer 3 Alex Langa standing by on the ramp to intercept her, but it was too late. The ambulance carrying the wounded soldier and our Flight Medic disappeared heading for the hospital.

"Let's just go without her, man." Wilson made the decision, got Vaughn back aboard, and spun the aircraft backward, heading to the active runway. That was the start of a very long morning shuttling patients between FOB Gamberi and J'bad. We raced back and forth picking up all the patients we could carry and finally collected Bringloe on one of the trips. She was exhausted and running on adrenaline like the rest of us by the time we landed on our last flight just before lunch.

It was comparatively quiet on the flight line now that the casualties had been handled, so we hovered over to refuel, then parked and shut down the aircraft. We unstrapped, recovered our weapons and then headed for the CP. While filling out the paperwork, Bringloe approached with a smile for the poor newbie pilot who was having an interesting first duty day flying with 4th Platoon. "How about that for a first mission?"

She toted up the numbers and let me know we'd evacuated 42 patients. She had no current information on how many survived, but it was enough at that point to know we'd given them a good shot at staying alive. No one was particularly hungry, but it seemed like a good idea to refuel our bodies as well as our aircraft.

"First-up's going to chow," Wilson transmitted on his handheld radio and we staggered toward the food.

"Hurry up!" A man from the second-up crew looked up from the videogame he was playing. While we were eating, they were on call.

We picked through the buffet line and I watched Vaughn contemplate a heaping plate of nasty fried chicken. "You gonna eat that garbage?" Vaughn thought it over, rubbing at the indentations from his helmet ear cups still visible on the side of his head, and turned his attention to a huge dollop of ice cream in a to-go cup. He decided on the ice cream and carried it outside. As the rest of the crew finished we all met up outside, thinking about what we'd been through that morning. We never got to eat in the chow hall, or even shower while on duty. At Shank we would even go 14 days without a shower; however, JAF was different, and you could get one every three days. But when big missions were going down, I didn't even take off my boots.

"Dude, that LZ was crazy, man." Flight Surgeon Ledlow was still charged with adrenaline. "Chill did an awesome job." We stood around eating and talking for a while as the second-up crew went to chow. It wasn't long before we got another mission. I ate a little food as we walked back toward ops for the brief and drank two bottles of water. I grabbed a third one, wrapped it in a wet sock to keep it cool, and stuffed it in a pocket. We had a patient waiting on the ground somewhere out near the Pakistan border, so we suited up in our sweaty gear and headed for the flight line.

We spooled up and brought the Blackhawk airborne into a clear sky over J'bad. We were headed for a little point that I'd penciled in on the map. As we approached the site, I looked out my door and stared into neighboring Pakistan. It was hard to tell exactly where the border was, and it certainly didn't seem to matter to the people on the ground clustered around makeshift field camps. Pakistani soldiers stood on

the other side of a tall ridgeline that ran through the rugged
mountains in this area. At least I thought they were Paki-
stanis. For all I knew they could be Talibs in one of their
sanctuaries. The LZ was just off our nose as we lost altitude
for the approach, but we couldn't see anyone waiting down
below for our arrival.

"Where are these dudes?" Wilson wondered out loud as
we dropped toward a pinnacle that the map said was the spot
for us to land. Once we were down on that little spot, it would
be impossible to see the ground and that reminded me of how
much I hate heights. That sounds silly coming from an aviator who spends most of his time in the air, but it was a weird
quirk with me that I didn't talk about much for obvious reasons. Unless I'm personally at the controls of an aircraft,
heights are bothersome to the point of distraction. I even get
vertigo sometimes when I walk into a room with high ceilings and look up. As Wilson made a slow approach, I
watched for the escort ship flying behind us and thought
about the time when my wife had me cleaning the outside of
our chimney.

I was up on the roof for maybe ten minutes, getting diz-
zier by the second and finally decided I'd had enough of being high off the ground minus an aircraft. She harassed me
about the irony but it didn't change my attitude. Unless you
are personally at the controls of an aircraft, heights are just
plain wrong and I hate them. I spent most of the approach
sucking in big gasps of mountain air as Wilson brought us
down with just one wheel balanced precariously on the small
pinnacle. We were stuck there, vibrating like clowns on a
unicycle until somebody delivered our patient.

Then I saw something that still sticks with me. There
were maybe six or seven soldiers on this isolated peak, miles
and miles from friendly units, occupying an observation post

that overlooked Taliban infiltration routes from Pakistan. They looked like lost children on a nature hike that had decided to set up camp and wait for someone to find them. I forgot about heights and felt a sincere reverence for the guys who caught this kind of mission and did it without complaint. If they got into serious trouble, help was a long way off and they had only their individual weapons and courage to fight through. Given what these guys manning this remote outpost must have felt, I had no business thinking about being scared.

We picked up the wounded man and careened off our perch with him sitting in the cabin nursing his broken ankle and staring at the mess of blood and gore from our missions into FOB Gamberi. Back at J'bad, we delivered the patient, gassed up the aircraft, and then shut it down. Crew chiefs were clustered all around us despite the mid-afternoon sun that beat down unmercifully on the pavement. They pulled a trailer containing a pressure washer up to the side of our aircraft and began to blow the clotted blood out of the cabin with streams of water. When they had the worst of it washed away, we all grabbed sanitary wipes and climbed into the cabin to do the detail work. There were certain things in the interior that we didn't want to get wet and there were splashes of blood on some of our equipment, so we usually handled this part of the clean-up as a crew. As we worked, I could see more of our 4th Platoon guys watching from the porch of the CP. They knew what we were doing; it was a routine for us all. I've looked up at fellow soldiers during these cleaning sessions and said things I never thought I'd say, like, "Hey, you've got some pieces of brains there on your shirt." They'd all had to deal with the evidence of bloody medevacs, and most of them simply watched us work, smoking cigars and wearing their black Stetson cavalry slouch hats to hide their eyes.

As we finished, I hopped down and saw a friend, Chief Warrant Officer 3 Matt Rudd—an Apache test pilot approaching from the hangar area where his aircraft was being repaired. He was talking to another Apache driver about an earlier mission during which Matt had caught a bad burst of ground fire. "Matt, how big was that round?" somebody shouted. Apache drivers flew heavily armed helicopters and were keenly interested in anything on the ground that had enough penetrating power to defeat their armor, thus bringing their flying days to an abrupt halt.

"Twelve-point-seven millimeter," Rudd responded with a grin. "It must have hit my dash. They're looking at it now." The conversation continued as he passed me with a nod. Thinking about getting hit in a relatively thin-skinned Blackhawk with a 12.7mm heavy machinegun got me to thinking about heights again and I turned to survey the mountains in the distance. The peaks that framed the mouth of the infamous Kunar Valley were clearly visible to the north with snow still covering their tops. There were a lot of 12.7mm heavy machineguns out there, and plenty of skilled Taliban gunners who loved shooting at American helicopters. There were just two weeks remaining before my mid-tour home leave, and I wanted very much to survive until then. Home with my wife, I hoped to forget blood, bodies, Afghanistan, and the Kunar Valley for a while—but it had affected me deeply and I knew forgetting would take more time than a short vacation at home.

Three weeks later, I was halfway through my leave, walking with Tess through an antique store in some little New England town, trying to enjoy a honeymoon that had been delayed for seven years by the back-to-back deployments. As we gawked at things, I caught a top-of-the-hour news report over the store's radio. It told of soldiers in Afghanistan's Kunar Valley sustaining heavy casualties during an operation called Strong Eagle. I tried to ignore it, but Tess knew me well enough to spot my subtle reaction. "Honey, isn't that where you are?"

"That's our area," I mumbled. My body was with my wife in New England, but my mind was with my fellow soldiers in the Kunar.

CHAPTER 3: REPLACEMENTS

**There are old pilots, and there are bold pilots,
but there are no old, bold pilots...”**
—Pilot's saying

Jalalabad, Afghanistan
7 June 2011

SERGEANT JULIA BRINGLOE was rummaging around in the medical container next to the pizza oven. The wooden door that was normally locked was braced open by a couple of boxes as she carried out a routine inventory of the 4th Platoon's medicines and medical gear. She could have used a hand with the chore, but the rest of the crew chiefs and flight medics were sprawled on the porch watching her work. It was typical of many of the men who worked with her on medevac flight crews. Some were not much more than teenagers. Julia didn't let immature behavior worry her. Beneath the banter and macho, she knew that most of them looked at her like an older sister and that pleased SGT Julia Bringloe.

She tolerated harmless hijinks most of the time, but when one of them stepped over her personal line, there was a rapid and firm reaction. She could offload discipline with a heavy hand when a situation called for her to straighten out a young trooper or obtain the respect she deserved as a noncommissioned officer. Julia was hardly thin-skinned, and she'd heard plenty of nonsense from men when she worked as a carpenter in Hawaii. That was before the Army, before Afghanistan, before she became a flight medic and a stalwart among 4th Platoon medevac crews.

She was born in Seattle and grew up Bainbridge, Washington, living with her mother and older brother. Always an active kid, Julia studied judo for years and became a champion swimmer in meets nationwide. There had been some serious emotional bumps on the road but she'd survived them all, including a terrible time as a kid when her Mom's best friend's husband had killed himself with a shotgun. For some unfathomable reason, Julia had been ordered to help clean up the mess left by the suicide. All traces of wide-eyed innocence ended that day.

Julia's father was around for part of her childhood, but he was distracted working long hours at a maritime engineering firm, so she never got much in the way of coaching or counseling from him. While still in high school, she began living on the street, couch-surfing with friends. She was eventually sent to a boarding school in Hawaii, where she finally found the structure she'd been missing at home and became president of the student body in her senior year. By the time she finished high school, Julia had developed into a strong young woman in charge of her future and looking forward to getting out on her own.

After a brief stint at the University of Idaho, she went back to Bainbridge and began working as a construction laborer to pay the bills, spending the next several years bouncing around from job to job, all over the country. She met her first husband and had a son named J.J. The couple worked together as carpenters, but eventually split. Bringloe worked next as a labor foreman for a large residential construction company. She met her second husband—also a carpenter— but she was tiring of the construction trades and longed for something more challenging. She had surgery for a damaged shoulder that kept her out of work for six months and it gave her some time to contemplate her situation. By the time she was fit to return to work, she knew it wasn't the pain that made her uncomfortable. It was the job that she hated. Julia wanted a new direction.

Bringloe was fascinated by helicopters and keenly interested in the work being done by outfits like Life Flight, a private firm that flew state-of-the-art aircraft and employed medical and aviation professionals to save critically ill or injured people by getting them to expert help. For a while, she followed Life Flight missions in her car or on foot, trying to learn more about what they did. It wasn't long before she understood she wanted to be a part of an effort like that. To make that happen, Julia Bringloe needed some training, some experience. That brought her to an interview with an Army recruiter.

The recruiter was honest with her. He couldn't promise a flight medic assignment directly after basic training, but if she was willing to train as a ground medic, there was a slim chance she could work her way into a flying assignment. The recruiter was also honest about what the U.S. Army was doing at the time. She would likely end up doing at least one combat deployment. That didn't faze Julia. She'd been over some rough roads and combat was just another ordeal she'd need to handle like she had so many other things in her life. She signed the line and headed for basic training as a 34-year-old private in the United States Army.

She did tours in Germany and Iraq where she thrived and earned a reputation as a loyal soldier and a capable medic. She applied for flight medic training and was accepted for a billet with the 10th Combat Aviation Brigade at Fort Drum, New York. She found a job she liked and a unit that treated her with respect as a soldier and a medical professional. As a Sergeant and qualified flight medic, Julia deployed with her unit to Afghanistan. She'd done a lot of flying and life-saving since then, sometimes hanging over sheer cliffs to pull wounded soldiers into her helicopters. It was just such a mission that earned her an Air Medal with V device denoting valor on a combat mission. Julia Bringloe—or B-Lo as she was mostly called around the unit—was treated with respect in the 4th Platoon and she liked the company she kept.

She was an avid foodie and often spent hours on the porch of the Command Post with fellow chow-hounds like me and Langa talking about food and recipes. She knew a lot about home repairs and renovations, which made her a popular source for advice. Julia was a heavy cigarette smoker who always claimed she was going to quit her pack-a-day habit and never did.

She was blowing smoke out from under her Cavalry Stetson set low on her eyes against the afternoon sun when she'd finished inventorying the medical gear in the storage locker. Sitting next to me in one of our homemade wooden porch chairs, she asked if I knew where our crew chief, Specialist David Capps might be. Capps was in Julia's squad, and she always liked to know where her people were and what they were doing.

"He's over in the ALSE shop working on gear," I said. Capps often did maintenance work on Aviation Life Support Equipment used by the flight crews, although it wasn't his Army-specified job. In this case, no one was available to check and repair the gear, so Capps just volunteered and went along to take care of it. It was typical of him.

David Capps was from Manchester, New Hampshire, a tall wiry guy who wore dark-rimmed glasses above an infectious grin. He joined the Army in 2006, specifically to work on helicopters. He was good at that and a lot of other mechanical things. He was also calm and unflappable to the point that we sometimes wondered if he ever understood the concept of risk or danger. Calm and cool behavior was a genuine asset for a man who lived the hectic life of a Dustoff crew chief, and I was more than a little happy to have him on my crew.

Capps was recently married, and his wife had joined him at Fort Drum after his first deployment to Iraq, where he worked arduous 12-hour days maintaining, repairing, and rebuilding Blackhawks. He loved working on aircraft, but he got a real charge out of riding in the birds he kept in prime condition. He kept pushing for a flight assignment and finally got a promise of flight status just before we deployed for Afghanistan. When we went overseas, David Capps left a pregnant wife behind on her way to live with relatives in Nebraska. He hoped the Army might get him home in time for the birth of their first child, but he never let that distract him from duties at his first assignment at Bagram Air Base. As a new guy replacement, he had a lot to handle. As it is in practically every Army outfit, new guys get a heavy workload and a lot of grief from old hands. David had to endure that and do a good job if he wanted to get into flight training—and he was not about to lose track of that dream.

Army helicopter crew chiefs do a lot more fixing than flying, but David Capps kept his head in the game and worked hard on aircraft maintenance. He worried about the duties he would be asked to perform when he finally became a crew chief. On flight status, he would be the only trained mechanic on any mission, the only one who knew how to fix it when something broke on the ground or in the air. No one else on the crew could do what he did, not the flight medic and not the pilots. David understood that and he worked hard to keep his aircraft airworthy at all times.

About mid-tour, the Army sent David home so he could be there for the birth of his son Hunter. He was proud and happy when he got back to Bagram and was ordered to the 4th Platoon at J'bad. There he would finally begin crew chief training. He arrived around the end of January and started to fly with medevac crews. He was still undergoing OJT when I met him and learned he would be flying on my crew. Capps was the only crew chief at J'Bad that had not done a combat hoist—one of the most difficult and demanding requirements for a fully qualified crewmember on medevac helicopters.

We had a status board in the ops office that tracked combat hoists, and David's name was the only one on the board that didn't have a hoist to its credit. He talked about it sometimes, wondering if he'd be able to operate the hoist and the Jungle Penetrator capably when his time came. It was a tough task to learn on the fly. Once the crew chief had the flight medic on the JP, their lives depended on the skill and courage of the man manipulating the hoist controls. Even if everything went right, a slow hoist up or down exposed the medic and patient to enemy ground fire for too long. There was always the possibility that the JP dangling below the helicopter could snag something and put the entire aircraft in jeopardy. It was also likely that he'd be called upon to assist the medic once the patient was on board with CPR or other lifesaving tasks. David Capps worried about all those things and secretly wished that he'd never have to do a combat hoist. But he was a "crew dog" in an outfit flying regular battlefield medevacs in difficult terrain—so he was not likely to escape the challenge.

It didn't help matters when Dan Fittos, the crew chief who lived with David in a hooch at J'bad, returned with a horror story about a hoist mission during which the aircraft had taken over a dozen bullets, the tires shot full of holes only inches from his dangling feet. It was a bad deal all around. The flight medic was shot several times while riding the hoist that Fittos controlled. The medic took a round through his knee and another which missed his liver by less than an inch. It wasn't the first or last aircraft or medic to have been shot during a hoist in our platoon. David Capps was waiting on the ground when the damaged Blackhawk staggered back into J'bad spewing hydraulic fluid. It was forced to land on mattresses to cushion the landing shock on a badly damaged airframe.

Capps and Bringloe were often my crew in the back of my helicopter flying medevacs out of J'bad. Flying up front with me at this point—about mid-way through our deployment—was sometimes our Platoon Senior Instructor Pilot or SP, the guy responsible for evaluating all the other pilots' knowledge and performance. The SP for 4th Platoon was Aaron Michaud, a bodybuilder with a thick Bostonian accent, and one of the finest Blackhawk drivers I'd ever met. When Aaron left the unit for his mid-tour leave, we were all sorry to see him go and a little concerned about who was going to fill his seat up front. I was already a fully qualified PC or pilot-in-command, but we were moving into fighting season, so I wanted another good instructor pilot around to learn from. I was delighted when the CO told me we would be getting Chief Warrant Officer 4 Kenny Brodhead to temporarily replace Aaron Michaud. Lots of people in the Blackhawk community knew Kenny and respected him. I was one of those, and over the years I'd learned a fascinating backstory about him, the Army, Blackhawk helicopters, and Dustoff in particular.

Brodhead was born to teacher parents in Florida and he was a musical prodigy from an early age. He could play practically any instrument and in grade school he had turned into a virtuoso on the tuba of all things. He endured being taught by his mom and dad through elementary and high school, where he was selected as a first-chair tuba player in the Florida All-State Band. While he was doing the musician gig, he met a girl named Josette, daughter of a senior NCO at Homestead Air Force Base that would later become his wife—but that was down the road a bit, and Kenny Brodhead had big plans before he thought about marriage. He wanted to see Europe. So he joined the Army as a musician, aced the audition, and spent a tour marching under a tuba with an Army band in Germany.

On a Christmas leave, Kenny ran into Josette again, but it was awkward at best. She didn't recognize him as Kenny Brodhead, the gawky, long-haired band nerd that she remembered. This guy had lost about 50 pounds and about a foot of greasy hair. This guy was a soldier at the wheel of an '87 Grand Am and she was smitten. They were married and planned to start a family as soon as Josette finished junior college.

During deployment for Operation *Desert Shield/Desert Storm*, Kenny got his first ride in a helicopter and suddenly decided there might be more to soldiering than playing in the band. He began to mumble about applying for flight school. While stationed at Fort Benning, Brodhead jumped out of airplanes during the day and worked a second job at Walmart during his off-duty hours. He used some of the extra money to pay for flying lessons in a little Cessna 172 light aircraft. Soon, he had both his private pilot's license and orders to

Fort Rucker, Alabama, for formal Army helicopter flight training. This was in early 1995, and before Kenny could climb into any kind of helicopter, he had to become an officer. That meant eight tough weeks at Warrant Officer Candidate School which involved lots of stress and running around in circles on the ground as prelude to lots of stress and running around in circles in the air.

Kenny made the grade and began flight training with lots of other Wobbly One Army warrants aspiring to be helicopter pilots at Fort Rucker. He quickly learned that hovering a helicopter—one of the first tasks required—is a lot like riding a unicycle on top of a bowling ball while juggling three rabid raccoons and reciting the alphabet backwards while you're half-drunk. There is nothing intuitive about controlling a helicopter. Both hands and both feet are simultaneously performing independent yet collaborative functions. Despite those demands and probably because Kenny Brodhead wanted it so much, the Army gave him the keys to a Blackhawk. He and Josette were both very happy about his new job and about the twins that were on the way to the Brodhead family.

Kenny liked Blackhawks a lot. They were eight tons of noise and vibration that could speed through the air at up to 200 miles per hour and then somehow screech to zero. He discovered that the Blackhawk can lift a truck, survive brutal punishment, and still deliver the crew safely back home. As his flight hours and skills grew, the Army sent Kenny Brodhead to a number of assignments. He spent a tour in Hawaii and then got orders to Fort Irwin in California's Mojave Desert. When Josette went into labor, Kenny rushed her to the local Army hospital where doctors decided mother was very sick and the babies were in distress.

At first light on the morning after Josette was taken to the hospital, the Army loaded her up on a medevac Blackhawk and rushed her to a bigger hospital. She underwent an emergency caesarean section and delivered twin boys. It was an ordeal. The boys were well underweight and had to be resuscitated several times. Everyone survived and Kenny decided he owed that good fortune to Army medevac flight crews. "The first-up medevac crew that flew them there was the key to their survival," Kenny often said. "I have a family because of a medevac helicopter and crew. I will never be able to repay that debt."

It didn't keep Kenny Brodhead from trying. After a stint teaching at Fort Rucker's flight school, he volunteered for medevac units and did several deployments flying Blackhawks to rescue soldiers on various battlefields. On his first deployment to Iraq, Kenny was at the controls of the medevac bird that rescued the first quadruple amputee to survive such horrific wounds. "It is hard to see people who are having the worst day of their life over and over again," Kenny told me. "But I tell my guys that we have to be at our best when that other guy is at his worst." With motivation like that, Kenny Brodhead was going to be a good man to have around.

So what about that other guy up front in a Blackhawk flying Dustoff out of J'bad in the summer of 2011—namely me?

When I was growing up, my mother worked a lot, so I spent time with my grandfather in Staunton, Virginia. He was a World War II veteran and I got my love of the military from him. I was a typical American kid for that time and place. I played sports, dabbled in music, and went away to college. And then I joined the Navy as a part-timer in the Reserves. I was independent and also homeless at the time, and Navy basic training was a solid shot at good, regular meals and a low-rent place to sleep for the summer. I survived the experience and returned to Virginia, where I promptly partied my way out of school and supported myself in very frugal style by playing gigs with local bands. I also did time as a roadie, bartender, butcher, and music teacher. I still have friends from that period who have become very successful professional musicians.

I moved to the West Coast and parked myself up around Mendocino in Northern California. I lived like a mountain man, off the grid, with no electricity or running water for a couple of years, just floating through life. Suddenly, it was September 11, 2001 and the world was changed by 19 *al Qaeda* terrorists who hijacked some commercial airliners and flew them kamikaze-style into Manhattan's Twin Towers and the Pentagon. When the body-count came in at over 3,000 innocent people killed, I knew what I had to do. I re-enlisted in the reserves, left California, and headed home to Virginia. While I was waiting for a chance to get back on active duty, I met my wife Tess. We got married and I got tired of waiting around, so I joined the regular Army instead, with a dream of becoming a helicopter pilot. My wife gave me purpose and I had a goal that I intended to make a reality.

The recruiter told me I was too old for flight training and I believed them. He got me to join as a helicopter mechanic and I went through boot camp again, by accident. I didn't let it phase me though. I went off on my first deployment to Iraq still scheming to game the system and work my way into flight school, hoping to become a meat servo. Tess had more faith than I did. She wrote me a note in lipstick on our bathroom mirror the morning I was scheduled to leave that said, "My husband will be a pilot!" Her confidence in me is what saved me from giving up on flight school. I was hard-headed now if nothing else. In Iraq, I once refused to go to a bunker during a rocket attack because I was filling out one of my interminable applications for flight training. I was rejected five times in a row. After I had been forced to land one day with a bad engine, and nearly got rolled up by some unfriendly locals, I must have performed well as our co-pilot Major Kline went to bat for me and got a general officer to forward a recommendation for one decidedly old applicant. Soon I returned from Iraq. I finally had orders to report to Fort Rucker for Warrant Officer Candidate School and Flight School.

It was a tough time for the Army in general and Army aviation in particular. Just two weeks after I got my orders for flight school my good friend from basic training Angelo Vacarro, a medic serving with the 10th Mountain Division, was killed by an RPG while he was shielding wounded with his body. He was highly decorated—and also dead, leaving behind two Silver Stars for his grieving wife. Several of my old buddies from the 101st Airborne were later shot down in Afghanistan and had to kill and evade the Taliban after their crashes. Still, I was determined to fly in combat. Tess was supportive but I was torn by what I'd seen. I was offered a deployment-free assignment in California, but I felt like a slacker even considering the offer. I turned it down and I too joined the 10th Mountain Division, who were already in Iraq. Tess just accepted the inevitable and dug in at home to survive a year without her husband. A blizzard was blowing when she dropped me off for the trip overseas.

Flying in combat in desert conditions is a whole new animal no matter what you've done in a helicopter before that. I learned all about dust landings, the Army aviation equivalent of a Navy carrier landing that provides a similar pucker-factor. It's as close as you ever want to come to being out of control while landing a helicopter. You're essentially blinded by the dust raised by your rotor wash as you come into ground effect. You simply pick a spot and announce something like "commit, commit, commit" as you drive the helicopter and crew into a huge brown cloud. It's a controlled crash. If you go too slowly, you brown-out with no way to tell if you're right side up or wrong side down. If you go too fast, you'll hammer the aircraft into the ground and break everything that should remain intact. There are no references or signals to help and the folks in the back can't see any better than you can from the cockpit. You mainly just keep descending and watch the wall of dust race up to engulf you like a big brown tsunami. You quite literally "feel" your aircraft into the ground.

During a dust landing, the ICS goes nuts, and you hear indecipherable things that sound like "lightdustatthetail-transition-mywindowyourdoorcleardownleaftandright!" It's someone in the back trying to help, but it doesn't mean much when you're straining to find just one little patch of ground for reference before everything disappears and you brace for impact. In daylight, it's intense. At night, it's terrifying.

It was about the time when I got back to Fort Drum from Iraq—and got transferred to Dustoff—that I first ran into Kenny Brodhead and Julia Bringloe. They sent me to Dustoff training and Kenny was the IP who gave me a check-ride or an evaluation flight. I was already a PC, but Dustoff was the big leagues. Bringloe was in the back laughing as Brodhead put me through some interesting paces. At the pre-flight brief, I told Kenny that I would take care of everything myself and he could kick back. He raised an eyebrow but shrugged and left to check the weather. I'd heard about

Kenny Brodhead and should have known I was making a mistake, but here I was an experienced combat flier returning from Iraq so what was he going to pull that I couldn't handle? I looked outside at the setting sun and tried to guess at what he'd throw at me tonight.

We were flying above upstate New York in fine shape until I shot my first approach to a nearby airport. Kenny reached for the throttles and shut one of our engines down to idle. "Whoops," he said. "You've just had one engine shot out. What now, sport?"

While I was trying to decide, Brodhead pressed some buttons and the helicopter started to porpoise in mid-air. "Now look at that," he said over the ICS. "It seems a rocket has blown away all your hydraulics." I was scrambling to correct our configuration when he hit another set of switches and we pitched nose down, headed for the ground with warning sirens blaring in my helmet. "Bad to worse," Kenny said. "You just lost your stabilator!" That wasn't enough for Kenny. He looked over at me, hit more buttons and decided we'd also suffered tail rotor damage. "Tail rotor is all shot up. Better roll it in fast because you won't be able to hold a hover. You're varsity now, pal. Deal with it."

I was sweating bullets. Kenny made everything go wrong and turned this check-ride into a pilot's worse nightmare. The runway was rushing up at us like the green wall at Fenway. Somehow I managed to maintain control and get us on the ground smoothly. Kenny repaired the simulated damage by flipping a few switches and then coached me through some of my mistakes. He seemed satisfied with my performance under pressure and let me do a few low-level pirouettes down the length of the runway to check my touch on the controls.

The ordeal was nearly over, but we still had to get back home through a descending layer of dark and what looked like icy soup from a weather front that was blowing rapidly into the area. We got airborne and were quickly blinded by the mush blowing in from Lake Ontario. It was so thick that we could barely see anything outside the cockpit. It was suddenly an all-instruments check flight. In conditions like this—what aviators call Inadvertent Instrument Meteorological Conditions or IIMC—it's easy to fly right into the ground. Seventy percent of all IIMC situations encountered by aircraft in flight, wind up with fatalities.

My heart was pumping way too fast as Kenny got on the radio to let the local air controllers know we were headed home. "Approach Control, Army Copter two six niner five is currently two miles west of Watertown airport, climbing through one-thousand-five-hundred for two-thousand. Request vectors for the Instrument Landing System approach into Wheeler Sack Army Airfield, full stop."

I dialed in all my settings and locked my eyes onto the instrument panel. I was intensely focused on the vertical situation indicator and the glideslope indicator that would guide me to the ground blindly at 120 knots, with only a few needles to watch. There was a jolting amount of turbulence that bounced us all over the sky and I had my doubts about whether or not I could get us back on the ground safely.

There was some discussion on the radio that indicated we might have to abort our return to Wheeler and find another airport farther away, but I was determined to try and get us back on home turf. At Kenny's request, Wheeler Army Airfield had their runway lights turned up to full-bright, but we couldn't see a thing below us as we chopped along on the heading the instruments said would take us home. I shook it all off and focused on controlling the aircraft, anticipating which direction the winds would try and push us next. Pitch and roll were perfect, power was good, and my descent was smooth in spite of the weather trying to push us off course. The altimeter continued to drop. We were close.

"I still can't see the runway, Erik," Kenny said. He was having some serious doubts, but I stayed on the instruments and tried to keep my focus. After a few minutes of gut-wrenching tension, I heard Kenny's voice. "I see the lights," he said. "I have the controls."

I took my sweaty hands off the controls and looked up to see a faint glow forming in the muck below us. Kenny kept us in a smooth descent and the haze melted to the point where I could finally see the ground. He slowed our descent and the helicopter bucked like a racehorse being reined in from a gallop as he bled off airspeed and set us up for landing. I took a couple of deep breaths and tried to convince myself it was no big deal, but we all knew better. It was a closely run thing, demanding superlative airmanship, and I had somehow pulled it off. Kenny seemed satisfied and let me know he thought I had done a good job on the controls during planned and unplanned emergencies.

While we were rolling back toward the hangars, I thought about the pre-flight sequence when I told Kenny that I would handle everything myself. Part of that was checking the weather and I'd left that up to him. He knew we might encounter some nasty conditions, but if the pilot says he's got it covered—well, Kenny was willing to see how that played out and maybe teach me a little lesson about proper mission planning. I vowed never to let something like that happen again as we shut down the engines and called it a routine night for Army aviators.

All that was a long time behind me as the unit prepared for deployment to Afghanistan. Leaving this time—a third deployment in just five years—was going to be tougher on me and on Tess. We were active in our church, but she had just a few friends to keep her company besides Lady, a small dog we'd rescued when I was in flight school. When the day came to say goodbye, we stood with the other soldier families as the busses rolled up to take us on the first leg of our journey to Afghanistan. Everyone wanted to squeeze in a last hug and kiss before that final tearful moment when we all piled aboard and headed off into the unknown.

If there was ever a better than average chance of my not making it home from a combat deployment, this was it, but I did what I could to reassure Tess. We stood wrapped in each other's embrace until the First Sergeant's voice echoed across the concrete telling us all it was time to go. As we boarded the buses, Tess was crying and I was doing my best not to. Tess looked me right in the eyes, and with a deadly serious tone, said, "Erik, do whatever you have to do." Everyone strained at the windows for a last look and then we were gone. Being deployed feels like being sentenced to prison. You feel condemned at that moment when you have to tell your best friend goodbye for the last time. You grasp each other's hands, you strain for one last glimpse, and wonder, *Will I ever see her again? Is this really worth it?* Because there is no guarantee that you will see her again, ever. You're the one who chose this life. You chose to make both of you feel this pain. You question yourself and your priorities. And then you shut off all the doubts and fears, because if you don't, you might not make it back at all. You are a soldier, and she understands. Even if nobody else in the world gets it, she does. It's time to go.

It was a long trip into the combat zone and I don't remember much between departure and when I woke up in Kyrgyzstan, where I got my first look at the Hindu Kush, the range of mountains that we would soon cross bringing us to our duty in Afghanistan.

Much of that was a distant, distracting memory by June 2011, the tail end of our Afghanistan deployment. We were in the home stretch. It did no one any good to countdown days remaining in the combat zone, but practically everyone did it anyway. Assuming I made it through whatever surfaced until we were relieved by another outfit, I would be heading to Fort Rucker for duty as an IP or Instructor Pilot. To be an instructor, an Army Aviator needs to be at the very top of his game. I was hoping Kenny Brodhead would give me a leg up on passing that ordeal while we were flying in the sandbox. It probably wouldn't be much of an imposition on his time as Kenny had recommended me for the assignment. Both of our reputations were at stake. Assuming a relatively quiet stretch over the next few weeks, I would do everything possible to fly with him. And when that happened, I would personally check the weather.

Life was as good as can be expected for a medevac pilot in a combat zone. It looked like all downhill from here. Of course, this was the Army, this was aviation, and this was Afghanistan—and there were a lot of bumps in that downhill road.

CHAPTER 4: H-HOUR

"No battle plan survives contact with the enemy."
Military maxim

17 June 2011

"Is that mission gonna happen, Sir?" Specialist Burt, one of Johnny Reyes' ops guys, was enjoying a post-dinner stretch in the break area outside our CP. I just shrugged and took another look at the maps. Who knew what the 3rd Brigade of the 25th Infantry Division would do now that they'd replaced the fabled 101st Airborne Division as the primary infantry unit covering the Kunar Valley? There had been indications for weeks that the Tropic Lightning soldiers were getting set to make their mark with the Taliban unit crawling all over the little peaks and valleys of that meat-grinder AO.

"If it does happen," I said, "things might get a bit busy around here."

Burt, Reyes, and all the other ops soldiers would know about it long before those of us in the medevac flight crews did. Manning the computers and radios, they got real-time intelligence. "I don't know, Chief." Burt ran a hand through a thick crop of dark-brown hair and cocked his eyebrows at me, a dead ringer for a taller John Belushi. "Those guys haven't really pushed into the valley like the hundred-and-first guys did. Maybe they're just getting used to the AO, you know? But they're giving the bad guys time to improve their foxholes." He yawned and went back to work at the computers. Burt wanted to get this deployment over with and get home. Like a lot of other young enlisted guys in our outfit, Burt saw the Army as a life experiment. He had no plans to reenlist and let everyone know that when his time was up, he was going to go to college in Colorado and become a Park Ranger. Beyond following the action on maps and computers, what happened in the Kunar Valley beyond our part in flying medevacs up there was not a big deal in Burt's life.

I spent many late nights in the quiet of the CP with Burt, usually when I was waiting for a good time to call Tess back in New York. With little to do during those nights when the place was as quiet as a desert truck stop, I studied the maps on the walls of the CP which showed both friendly and enemy dispositions. Back when the 101st was handling the AO, those maps looked a lot different than they did now. The Screaming Eagles were an aggressive outfit. Late in their time patrolling the Kunar, a time when most units slow down to keep casualties to a minimum, the 101st did the opposite. They tore up through the valley and took the fight directly to the Taliban, daring them to step up for a bloody slug-fest. It didn't surprise me. I had seen them do it before in Iraq at the height of sectarian violence.

The 101st Airborne was my old outfit before I became an Army Aviator, and I still felt a kinship with them. In the big Army they were like licorice—you either hate it or you love it. I'd been quite happy with their style back at Fort Campbell, and they carried that street-fighter mentality with them into Afghanistan. But the Screaming Eagles were gone now, back home with their families in Kentucky. These days, the Kunar Valley was the responsibility of 3rd Brigade, 25th ID, and they were slowly getting a feel for themselves and the enemy.

To be fair, any outfit working in the Kunar had a tough patch to handle. The spider web of valleys that spun off the

Kunar to the north was only irregularly pressured by the Army high command. Tightly contested areas like the Korengal Valley—a finger running off the Kunar—were brutal battlefields that ate up men and material. They were pressed mainly to keep the wolves from larger doors elsewhere, and when the allied units left, the Taliban returned. Units regularly found themselves fighting over the same ground again and again, but it had to be done. It was the nature of the fight in Afghanistan. Even us non-infantry aviation pogues knew the best way to negotiate with a mortal enemy is to go over to his house, kick down his door, and punch him in the mouth while he's eating his Lucky Charms. It may be harsh, but it beats fighting in your backyard. The 25th Infantry Division now had the unenviable task of doing just that. And when they did, we'd have a lot of medevacs to handle.

On the day after my conversation with Specialist Burt, it seemed like the action might commence sooner rather than later. I overheard Captain Wilson talking with one of our pilots about an upcoming Air Assault. "Is this the mission we've been hearing about?" Wilson just nodded and told me to wait for the full Air Mission Briefing. Apparently that would not be long in coming. Nosing around further, I discovered that our Aviation Task Force Commander Lieutenant Colonel Downey was working on the details with the ground unit commanders. When they had a concept hammered out, they would gather the leaders of all the aviation units scheduled to fly and get specific about what was expected from flight crews.

Never one to be caught short of information, I cornered CPT Wilson later and asked him for a little heads-up on the medevac piece of the puzzle. "We might have to reposition up to Joyce to support the op," Wilson said. FOB Joyce was a remote operating base deeper up into the Kunar and not a pleasant place to spend your time.

"How long?"

"Not sure," Wilson responded thinking it over while he gazed at one of the maps on the wall. "A few days maybe—until they wrap it up." Next to the map was our flight schedule and it told me that I'd be flying in whatever happened up at FOB Joyce. Wilson saw where I was looking and pointed at the schedule.

"It'll probably be you and me as PCs, with Alex Langa and Smith as PIs." From my perspective as one of the scheduled command pilots that was not such good news.

Smith was a great guy, but he was fresh out of flight school. He'd had a lot of civilian flight experience, and was becoming an excellent helicopter pilot, but this was his first deployment and he didn't have much time flying combat missions. And this deal was going to involve some less-than-zesty missions given the area, enemy, terrain, and weather up there in the valley. It didn't seem fair to Smith or to the rest of us. We could do better. After thinking it over, I went back to CPT Wilson and laid it on the line with what I hoped was a convincing argument.

"Sir, I need a more experienced guy in my cockpit," I said launching directly into my case. "I don't think this is the best crew selection for an op like this one. It's not personal, but how about giving me somebody else?"

"Seriously?" Wilson didn't seem shocked with my reasoning or my complaining. "Why? Look, Sabby, if you don't think you can handle it I'll get you somebody else...but really?" He didn't wait for an answer and I was now apparently on the CO's hit list. CPT Wilson said he'd get back to me with a decision.

While I waited, I wondered if I'd done the right thing. Smith was OK and someday soon, with some more stick time, he'd be a fine, reliable aviator but this was bound to be a tough mission calling for all the experience at hand. As a pilot-in-command I owed it to the mission, the unit, my crew, and myself to try and get the best hand available where lives were on the line. It was my call and I'd made it based on my best judgment. Now it was up to the CO. He'd either back my request or tell me to carry out my orders and rub some dirt in it. I was miserable for a while, thinking about Capps and Bringloe in the back of the aircraft. Both of them were relatively new and adding a third inexperienced hand didn't seem like the best way to go.

The PI I really wanted was Chief Warrant Officer 3 Aaron Michaud, our platoon instructor pilot and one of the Army's best Blackhawk drivers, but he was on leave. I kept thinking about what Aaron told me just before he left. "Sabby, don't let them paint you in a corner while I'm gone. Do the right thing; don't take chances. This is fighting season. This is serious." The more I thought about it, the more I became convinced that I did the right thing, so I found CPT Wilson and asked for his decision. I knew Aaron would have backed me up.

"The commander said he was disappointed that you declined Smith," Wilson told me. He had a grin on his face, but I could tell it was tough on him also. He was the guy who would tell Smith that he had been passed on by his scheduled PC. "You're gonna fly with Kenny while he's here." I was a little shocked at the lack of argument or conversation. With Kenny visiting 4th Platoon to replace Aaron while on leave, I could probably get in some extra training if things were slow. But Wilson misread my reaction. "Don't tell me you're worried about flying with Kenny Brodhead! I'd fly with him anytime. Come on, Sabby. You're about to go be an instructor pilot at Rucker!" I quickly reassured him that I was more than fine with Kenny Brodhead as a PI, but Wilson wasn't about to let me off the hook right away. I laughed it off, knowing that he still had my back and probably took a chewing himself from his own boss.

"I don't know, man. The Major was kind of disappointed in your call on this." The unspoken message in that comment was that Captain Wilson had thought about replacing me rather than Captain Bonney. He could do that, and maybe even take the assignment himself flying with Kenny, but we both knew that was unlikely. He already had a great crew manning his aircraft that he wouldn't want to disrupt. Wilson flew with Vaughn, our best crew chief, and our senior Flight Medic Staff Sergeant Brian Cammack. Both had more combat hoists and flying experience than almost any crewmember in the entire company.

So I got off easy and I got what I wanted. And I got what was best for the mission and for the rest of my crew. If my ego was damaged a bit, so be it. It wasn't the first time in the Army when I'd been told a senior was disappointed in me. As long as regulations were followed and the mission was accomplished safely, that stuff rolled off my back. Being the old guy in the unit had advantages. *If this doesn't work out, I could always go back to being a butcher*, I told myself. While we waited for the ball to drop up in the Valley, I got in some pre-Instructor Pilot Course training with Kenny Brodhead.

There was tension in the air for the next couple of days. Everyone seemed to know the big operation was about to commence and speculated about just when it might happen, especially at morning briefings in the Task Force TOC or Tactical Operations Center. We found out about it on the morning when I was late out of my bunk and rushing to make time for a few minutes in the Pilot's Penthouse reading my Bible. When I finished, I cut through the CP, catching the previous night's duty crew cleaning up the office spaces. It was an all-hands deal, with officers giving the enlisted folks help with sweeping and mopping.

"How were the missions?" I asked one of the flight medics carrying a mop bucket outside. He just shrugged. "Couple of priorities and an urgent tib-fib fracture. IED." Seemed like just another routine night for medevac crews. I headed for the briefing room and paused before the door to read the sign posted there. *Somewhere, a True Believer is training to kill you. He is training with minimal food and water, in austere conditions, training day and night. The only thing clean on him is his weapon and he made his web gear. He doesn't worry about what work-out to do. His ruck weighs what it weighs and his runs end when the enemy stops chasing him. This True Believer is not concerned about how hard it is. He knows either he wins or he dies. He doesn't go home at 1700. He is home. He knows only The Cause. Still want to quit?*

Those words had had a big impact on me, and I usually took time to read them. I had never seen a better description of what we were facing in Afghanistan. The last of the winter snow was gone from the distant peaks. It was prime fight time.

The morning briefing was routine at first and we all sat around yawning and sucking on coffee cups. Weather was good but becoming marginal and satellite imagery of Asia showed vast swaths of cloud cover in huge swirling bands converging on Iran and heading for Afghanistan. We dealt with nightly recaps, daily assignments, and some other piddling matters. Then it got interesting.

"The Air Mission Brief is tonight after chow." Captain Wilson just laid it out there like any other standard drill. "All PCs will be at the brief. You can have your guys come or you can brief them later, but I'd have them there for it." It was what we'd been waiting for, and there was a rumble of conversation through the room.

"We'll bring everybody," I said to Kenny who was next to me jotting down call signs and frequencies on his kneeboard. "Best we have everyone singing from the same sheet of music." Kenny just nodded and smiled indicating he agreed with that decision. I turned aside to Kenny quietly. "Listen," I said. "Are you sure you don't want to be PC for this thing?"

"No way," he said and went back to his note-taking. "This is your AO. You know it better than I do. You're the man for the operation."

"Well, it's gonna be a long day before we find out what's in store for us up at Joyce."

"Relax, Sabby. If it's slow, we can use the time to get in some more training. I've got a couple of little cockpit tricks I can show you. I do it all the time with the guys I fly with." That was a nice gesture, but I suddenly had a distinct feeling we wouldn't have a lot of training time up at FOB Joyce.

For the Air Mission Brief, we were packed into the Tactical Operations Center like sardines. It was an all-hands, all-branches, all-airframes drill. Prior to the arrival of the formal briefers, we stood around trading names and experiences. Infantry officers talked with Apache and Kiowa pilots. Chinook drivers huddled to go over their transport mission packages. Blackhawk assault pilots poured over maps. Captain Wilson was over in a corner talking with some Air Force Search and Rescue pilots. The USAF Pararescue guys had come up to J'bad to cover the medevac mission while we repositioned to FOB Joyce supporting the 25th ID.

When a young captain designated the primary briefer stepped up to the front of the room and asked for quiet, we scattered and found seats. I slipped toward the back of the room, found one of the elevated desks, and began to leaf through the mission package that we'd all be handed when we arrived.

"Time is now 2300 Zulu," the captain announced as everyone raised their arms to synchronize their watches. "This is the Air Mission Briefing for Operation *Hammer Down*." There was a long and detailed rundown of all aspects of that from a series of briefing officers. They covered weather, intelligence, fire support, ground task force plan, insertion and pick-up details, and everything else crews flying helicopters in support of the 25th ID might need to know. A map in the terrain section of the briefing caught my eye. Most of the infantry insertions were at spots along a high ridgeline, listed at well above 10,000 feet. That might make holding a hover in thin air difficult. I made a note to check it when Kenny and I went flying tonight. The predicted ambient temperatures in the Watapur Valley were scorching, and they wouldn't be much cooler high up. Heat was another problem that often kept our Blackhawk's engines from producing sufficient power when it was most needed. There are three things you don't want to be in any aircraft: Too high, too heavy, or too hot. We might be all three. Super.

The infantry guys gave us the basic intent of Operation *Hammer Down*. Units from the 25 ID's 2nd Battalion, 35th Infantry Regiment were going to land up on those ridges and then sweep down into the valley with the objective of destroying a cooperative Al Qaeda and Taliban base camp. It was the same type of mission that seemed to happen every year at one place or another in the Kunar Valley. The grunts would hit the base camps, kill some Taliban fighters, and then depart for a mission somewhere else. Shortly after they departed, the Taliban would come back and another base camp would be established. It was like Groundhog Day— déjà vu all over again.

This time, the infantry was going deeper into the valley and everyone was a little shaky about a lack of vehicle support in the initial assault. APCs, Strykers, and Armored Humvees wouldn't make it into the valley to catch up with the leg infantry, so our helicopters would be their only lifeline during the operation. *Well,* I thought as the briefing broke up, *if it was easy, anybody could do it.*

After dinner, we retreated to our rooms for the evening. I finished packing a small bag with some extra clothing, some shower shoes, towel and toiletries, my Bible, a picture of Tess, a sleeping bag, and my pillow. I had spent many nights on small, austere outposts and bases, far from the luxuries of the FOBs, and I knew to pack only the bare necessities.

I called Tess and talked for about a half-hour that night, grateful for the cheer and confidence in her voice. Things had changed significantly on the home front since my first deployment, and Tess was becoming an old hand at separation, or had at least convinced me of such. Thinking about her courage and devotion, it was hard for me to understand how my grandparents had handled it all during World War II when the men came home only after they were killed, wounded badly, or the war ended. "I'm going on a trip for a few days," I told her. "I might not be able to call. I'm not sure if this place has phones or not." *Probably not,* I thought silently. It was common knowledge that the Taliban might monitor some of our morale-phone circuits.

"How long will you be gone?"

"Not sure, really; but don't worry. I'll be fine." The rest of the time we talked about routine matters over here and back there. It was just conversation to hear each other's voices. I rarely missed a chance to call home and never minded waiting hours for my turn on the busy phone lines. We were a devoted couple and very much in love. As my time ran out, we read some scripture together and then I had to get moving. There were a lot of people waiting to call home before we launched in support of the operation in the Watapur Valley.

On my way back to the CP, I ran into Specialist Capps eating dinner. "You gonna call Sadie tonight, Capps?"

"I'm just hanging out, sir. Gonna call Sadie tomorrow."

"Tell her and Hunter hello from me." I left him chewing on a chicken leg and went to ops to check on how the 25th ID's insertions were going up in the valley. We had heard helicopters roaring overhead most of the day.

Specialist Burt was manning the ops desk, amid his computer screens and a constant buzz of SATCOM radio traffic. "They're already off, sir. No issues and no wounded so far."

"That's a relief," I said, eyeing the LZs again on the wall maps. But it was much too soon to predict a cakewalk for the troops up in those mountains. With nothing better to do before morning launch, I hung around ops until around 2200, hoping that the insertions would continue unopposed and without incident. There would be medevacs soon enough— either someone hit or someone with a broken bone in the rough terrain. We'd launch on anything like that. It set me to pacing and thinking about an old soldier's rule of thumb about combat deployments. The deadliest time is always at the beginning of a deployment or at the end of one. And we'd been deployed now for ten months.

When it was useless to stay awake any longer, I left the CP and made my way to the Pilot's Penthouse to try and get some sleep in the humid 90-degree night air. I didn't sleep long or very deeply, but that had nothing to do with the temperature.

I was awake at 0430 and grabbed my split-kit to head for the flight line. On the way, I passed Capps talking on the phone. He just grinned and showed me a thumbs-up. There was time yet before launch, and Capps would be there to do his duty. He always was.

Blackhawk 9-4-4 was ready for flight when I arrived. The maintenance crews had been busy during the night. The Hawk was freshly washed and its blotchy green paint was emblazoned with its number in white over a red cross. The same markings were painted in a white box on both cargo doors and the nose of the aircraft. Kenny Brodhead arrived next, and Julia Bringloe followed carrying her medical equipment. In a practiced routine, we tossed our gear into the bird and secured it to the cargo floor with D-rings and then waited aimlessly for Capps and the crew of 9-4-2, the other medevac bird slated for FOB Joyce. That one would be flown by CPT Wilson and CW3 Alex Langa with Vaughn and Cammack in the back as crew chief and flight medic respectively.

Alex Langa arrived on time as usual. The rest of his crew was scattered taking care of last-minute details. Alex was double-fisting coffee and trying to get them all organized for the scheduled lift. He waved at me and I grinned at his frustration. "It's like trying to herd cats, right Alex?"

"Oh, yeah," he said and rolled his eyes as he tossed his gear into the aircraft. "Lucky all I have to do is fly."

Flying is what Chief Warrant Officer 3 Alex Langa did best. He was my best friend at JAF, and along with Chief

Warrant Officer 3 Aaron Michaud, we'd formed a little mutual aggravation society we deemed the "Trifecta of Anger," a group of three sarcastic Warrant Officers determined to support each other and annoy everybody else.

Alex was from Argentina via Boston. He was short, stocky, and bald with a sarcastic aspect on life in general and the Army specifically. He was a former Marine Corps captain who left that service because they refused to train him to fly. The Marine Corps offered him promotion to major if he'd stick around, but Alex wanted something different so he joined the Army, qualified to become a warrant officer, went to Fort Rucker where he excelled, asked for Blackhawks, and then got his wings.

"I did what the Marine Corps told me to do," he told me once in the Pilot's Penthouse, "but it was paperwork and all the nonsense that comes with it. I'm happy being a warrant officer because we fly. That's our job first and foremost: to be experts at flying our aircraft." Among his other duties, Alex served as maintenance test pilot for our platoon of three aircraft. He personally flew each Blackhawk coming out of maintenance for one reason or another and none of them were declared mission-ready until Alex had taken them up and checked them out. He was a tough taskmaster on the maintenance troops. He was also in charge of our small stable of crew chiefs, and he treated them all like sons.

Five times our Blackhawks had entered maintenance due to battle damage from enemy ground fire, and Alex had been on most of those missions. He was known throughout the unit as our resident bullet magnet. Thanks primarily to the efforts of Alex and our platoon's crew dogs, throughout our deployment we'd never had to drop a single mission due to maintenance. I owed him a lot for a lot of reasons. It was Alex who served as my mentor and chief cheerleader when

I had some reservations about being ready for this deployment. He and Aaron Michaud taught me a lot about the Blackhawk, flying, and being an Army Warrant Officer.

Watching Alex climb around his helicopter while waiting for the rest of his crew to show, I thought about an earlier flight with him that had all the aspects of a disaster. We were coming back from a mission over J'bad, listening to a music radio station he'd found on one of our radios. There he sat, head bopping along with the tunes, when suddenly we began to lose the hydraulic pressure that powered our flight controls—a very bad situation in a helicopter. The master caution panel lit up like a Christmas tree and we declared an emergency as the airfield mustered fire trucks and a gaggle of spectators waiting for the crash. He set it down smoothly and just continued on with his day. No big deal.

Alex had a lot of stories like that. Earlier in the year his medic had been shot for the second time while riding the hoist on a mission as Alex fought the controls to save the bird. He'd suffered an RPG passing near his rotor disk, and he'd had a couple dozen bullet holes shot through his aircraft. He brought them all back, and he managed to gently land his leaking aircraft and blown up landing gear tires on mattresses without incident. Alex should have been given a few Broken Wings, an award for helicopter pilots that manage to save a badly damaged aircraft, repeatedly, but he wasn't interested in accolades. Alex was interested in flying and saving lives. He was a natural Dustoff guy.

He was also an excellent teacher. He was climbing into his seat in the Blackhawk across from ours, and I remembered another flight we'd taken just a few weeks ago when everyone had already finished running up, waiting inside for us to go to chow. "How about practicing some roll-ons in case we ever lose the number one hydraulic system?"

Alex stared at me curiously for a moment. We never did EP or emergency training on duty, but I'd had an almost otherworldly premonition—something was telling me to go practice that morning. I hoped Alex would agree even though it wasn't SOP.

"OK," he said, and took his hands off the controls.

We did several practice approaches, rolling the aircraft down the runway to perform the emergency procedures for landing minus hydraulics and using only our forward momentum to keep from spinning out of control with a damaged tail rotor. We took turns on the exercise, critiquing performance and offering tips on procedures. When we were nearly satisfied that we could handle the situation if and when it arose, I asked Alex to try for one more pass.

"You da' man, brother," I said. "I'll call you below sixty knots." In the Blackhawk, 60 knots groundspeed is officially the maximum speed the aircraft can handle at the point it touches the ground, though I had heard that it could handle much more if it had to from friends who had crash landed them before. Alex banked right, pulling back on the cyclic and jamming the stick to the inside of his right thigh. Keeping my hands off the controls, I followed along and watched as the clapping of our rotors drowned out the rush of wind coming through the open windows. It was the start of a roller-coaster ride.

"I'm starting my approach," Alex said calmly. There was nothing to see but sky in our windscreens as he bent the Blackhawk around and bled off airspeed. He turned the aircraft around like a NASCAR driver, and there was barely time to see anything zipping by us on the ground. In the back, our crew strapped in and locked their inertia reels. As Alex continued to muscle the controls, I felt the Blackhawk sink and braced for the tail wheel to slam into the ground. This was too much—a prescription for that bane of all helicopter pilots, the controlled crash. As I braced for impact, Alex deftly dialed in some collective with his left hand.

My voice on the ICS was a little short of calm as I shouted our status. "Fifty-nine knots; you're below sixty!" Alex had it covered all the way. The aircraft greased onto the runway with all three wheels touching down at once and we were perfectly lined up with the centerline of the runway.

"Three point landing," I croaked. "Very nice."

Alex just shrugged and keyed the radio. "Tower, Dustoff 7-2 is clear of the active. We will be repositioning to Medevac parking and termination." He sounded bored. And that was Alex—all the way, all the time. I was more than happy to have him in the lead aircraft flying out of FOB Joyce on this mission.

Right on time, all the crew members assembled on the morning we launched in support of Operation *Hammer Down*. Crew chiefs cleared the Auxiliary Power Units or APUs and we cranked the engines for checks prior to turning the rotor blades. In the back of my aircraft, Julia Bringloe checked her MBITR, a Multi-Band Inter-Team Radio that she would carry if and when she had to be outside the aircraft. Capps rotated the huge arm of the rescue hoist and unwound a large pile of cable, which Bringloe cradled carefully in her arms. He double-checked the controls on his pendant, taking a close look at the override switches and the rubber shock bumper that protected the cable where it wound into the hoist.

While that was going on in the back, I checked the emergency panel for the hoist located on a console between the cockpit seats. Nobody up in the cockpit ever used these backup controls for the hoist. The pilots couldn't really see what was happening in the back, so trying to control a combat hoist from up front would be a very dicey proposition, but the controls were there if remote operation was absolutely necessary. When we were satisfied that all systems were functional, I started the engines and saw the crew of 9-4-2 cranking up also. It was a leisurely, routine process. The insertions up in the mountains being carried out by the Blackhawk and Chinook crews were going along as planned, and there was nothing for us to do but get up into position and wait for a call. Kenny and I had agreed to set a relaxed tone—what Kenny called the "façade of confidence"—and treat this operation like just another day at the office. We checked in with CPT Wilson in the other bird and they called the tower.

"J-A-F tower, Dustoff 7-2 and Dustoff 7-3 are two UH-60s in Medevac parking, ready for takeoff, departure to the north."

"Dustoff 7-2 flight, you are cleared for takeoff to the west, right turn out to the north, winds two four zero at ten gusting to fifteen, altimeter setting 3-0-0-4, report alpha sector outbound." Cleared for departure to FOB Joyce, we lifted, dipped our noses to gain forward momentum, and accelerated past the concrete T-barriers that lined the FOB at J'bad while Wilson confirmed details with the tower.

"Altimeter 3-0-0-4—and we'll call alpha on the outbound for Dustoff seven-two flight." Wilson's voice was calm with a cheerful note. Apparently he and Alex Langa were also maintaining that façade of confidence. We were completely autonomous in our two Blackhawks, a self-contained unit, free from the flagpole as we rocketed over the city. Jalalabad rushed by beneath us in a blur of dirty streets, Arabic billboards, and flat sand-colored roofs belching black smoke. There was very little moisture in the air that morning, but what was there gave a brilliant orange aura to the rising sun. We picked up a course parallel to the river that runs into the Kunar and followed it toward the mouth of the valley. The mountains stretched like jagged fingers on either side of our flight as we headed for Joyce, a small fire base south of FOB Monti, named for another 10th Mountain solder who lost his life and received the Medal of Honor for his actions. There was no way of knowing it on that beautiful morning, but somewhere up on the side of one of those peaks, a 25th ID platoon was about to step into a deadly trap.

CHAPTER 5: MEDICS ON THE GROUND

> **If there must be trouble, let it be in my day,**
> **that my child may have peace.**
> –Thomas Paine

25 June 2011

"FOB JOYCE, FOB JOYCE, good morning. Dustoff 7-2 and 7-3 are inbound from the south."

Captain Wilson contacted our new temporary base and we followed his lead into a slow right roll setting up for an approach to the FOB helicopter landing area. We had some things to do before setting our aircraft on the ground, so the crew got busy.

"Sea-Moss is safe," I said and flipped a switch to deactivate our Common Missile Warning System (CMWS), the sensor device that protected us from missiles and helped give us a bit of audible warning if we got painted by one.

"Pin is in," Capps responded from the back as he installed the backup safety pin in a black box next to his radio controls. It didn't take a lot of concentration, and like the rest of us the crew chief was focusing on the landing area at FOB Joyce. As we approached, we could see a flat area about the shape of home plate on a baseball diamond. Joyce was scraped out of sand and scrabble, butted hard up against a steep ridge-line. As we circled to get a better feel for the area, I could see two steep, barren mountain ranges off to the east. Just below the peak of the closest high ground was a small

Afghan Army outpost. We could see lumps of sandbags surrounding a little mud hut with a green tarp roof and an Afghan flag blowing in the breeze.

Kenny was flying and he bent us around to the south, staying abeam of 7-2 as we descended on a smooth approach, headed for touch-down in a huge gravel expanse that was kept clear for helicopter operations. Joyce was a busy place, home for the soldiers operating now in the Watapur Valley, an off-shoot of the larger Kunar Valley, where Operation *Hammer Down* was now a few hours in progress. Joyce was a medium-sized fire base that was home to the soldiers who were now hiking down the Watapur Valley mountains. FOB Joyce had been constructed like virtually all Army operating bases in Afghanistan and dotted with Hesco barriers for blast protection. The Hescos were ubiquitous in the Sandbox—large rebar-reinforced cubes that were filled with dirt and scattered around bases to provide soldiers with handy cover against indirect fire attacks. The LZ we were approaching was about the size of two football fields, and beyond it were clusters of soldiers laboring over piled pallets of supplies for the troops working in the mountains above them.

We could see a row or two of rusty Milvan containers and some small housing structures with a snarl of antennae jutting up from flat roofs. There was some rubble from older Afghan structures, but the eye-catching feature was a huge sandbag mosaic that spelled out *Task Force Cacti.*

Our two Blackhawks touched down side by side and we began to shut down the engines, radios, and powered systems. We were home for however long the Army said and ready to fly in support of Task Force *Cacti*, the mission-oriented element of the 25th ID operating in the mountains surrounding the base. As the main rotor systems spun down, our crew chiefs and flight medics got busy on the ground. They were shuttling equipment into a structure off to one side of the LZ. That was likely FOB Joyce's aid station. We let them handle it and gathered out in the hot sun between our parked helicopters to contemplate what was next for our medevac detachment. It was hard to talk over the roar of a big Russian-made Mi-17 transport helicopter that was approaching the LZ with two large rubber blivets full of water suspended in a sling load. As the pilot brought his aircraft to a hover and maneuvered the load into position for the ground crews to unhook it, his rotor wash blew a storm of dirt and debris over us.

To get out of the blast, we walked to the aid station that would serve as our CP while we flew out of FOB Joyce. We needed to check in, report ready for duty, and get an update on what was happening up in the mountains. The FOB aid station was a large room with tall ceilings. There were multiple stretchers scattered amid a forest of IV trees and other emergency medical equipment. Beyond the operating area, a smaller room full of dusty couches was stacked with boxes of food and canned soda. There was even an old wide-screen TV set in one corner. This was the rec room for the people who ran the aid station—a kind of urgent-care clinic—at FOB Joyce.

Connecting the two areas was a galley or eating area containing folding chairs and tables. Our enlisted folks had commandeered several of the tables and were setting up their computers and comm gear. CPT Wilson found a secure phone and called J'bad to let them know we were safely on the ground. Our hosts from the Task Force *Cacti* medical detachment answered questions and moved things around to accommodate the space we needed. I asked a nearby soldier where we would be sleeping and eating. He volunteered to take those of us not busy getting set for operations to a sleeping tent.

As we walked out of the aid station, our crew chiefs Capps and Fittos were shoulder to shoulder engaged in their usual banter. "You know you're gonna get a hoist on this one," Fittos said. "So don't forget which button is up and which one is down."

Capps elbowed him sharply. "Right—and I'll try not to get my medic shot through the knee like you did." We might be at a new operating base, but not much had changed among the crews.

As we followed our guide toward a line of sagging, wind-blown general-purpose tents, we checked our radios to be sure we would be in touch no matter where we were at Joyce if a mission dropped. Our sleeping tent was typical for the area. It was dusty and hot, smelling of plastic and dirty feet. It had a plywood floor with tubular air-conditioner ducts suspended from the ceiling by Velcro straps. Naturally, there was no air, conditioned or otherwise, flowing through the ducts. I dropped my gear and poked my head outside to squint at another set of tents I spotted on the walk from the aid station. They looked decidedly better and would put our accommodations closer to our Blackhawks, so I made a mental note to check them out for availability later.

The mess hall was no great shakes; about what we had at J'bad and about what we expected. The food was…well, it was nourishing and likely a stretch better than what the guys up in the mountains were eating. When I'd eaten what I could, I walked back to the aid station to see if anything had happened that needed our attention. Our crews were sprawled around comfortably keeping an eye on things and

an ear tuned to the tactical radio nets. There was a more relaxed atmosphere this far forward and they seemed to appreciate that.

Captain Wilson was conferring with a female officer in
a corner of the room while SGT Johnny Reyes wandered
around making sure Fittos, who was drafted to be an Ops guy
for the mission, had what he needed. I walked over where
Reyes and Fittos were conferring on crew schedules. "Everything is chill, boss," Fittos told me. "Nothing yet."

I asked them to keep us updated on the radio and walked
back toward the sleeping tent. On the way, I scoped out the
port-a-johns and shower area. If it stayed this quiet, we might
just get some rest at FOB Joyce. I should have known better.

We were short of cots, so I laid out that night on the tent
floor next to Capps who was busy with a computer game. It
was hot and uncomfortable, but I was tired from staying up
most of the previous night, so sleep came after a few fitful
tosses. My last thought was of Tess. I wondered what she
was doing back in New York while I was trying to sleep in
a muggy tent so far off in Afghanistan. *Dear God,* I prayed,
*please keep us safe. Don't let me do anything to get us all
killed, and keep those guys on the mountain in your hands.*

The alarm went off seemingly seconds later. "Medevac,
medevac, medevac!" The tent flap blew open and one of our
ops soldiers shouted over the radio what we'd all been expecting.

We scrambled for our radios and checked in with ops to
let them knew the crews of both Blackhawks were awake
and headed for the mission brief. Eight of us chugged out of
the tent into scorching morning sunlight and took off running. My watch told me we'd gotten some sleep, which

meant we would be alert and rested for whatever was required. Captain Wilson and his crew chief barely beat me to the CP as a soldier was reading off the grid location where a wounded soldier needed air evacuation.

Kenny Brodhead took a quick look over my shoulder and then ran toward the LZ to get the helicopter prepped and started. Reyes handed me a copy of the nine-line medevac request. We had one soldier with shrapnel wounds at a remote location in the Watapur Valley area. CPT Wilson thought this might be the tip of the iceberg and decided we would lift both aircraft on this one. We got the rest of the brief and headed out to go flying.

Both birds were hissing like coiled snakes when we got to the LZ. We were ready to start. Opening the door on my side of 9-4-4, I dropped my body armor over my head, secured the Velcro, crawled into my survival vest, and jammed my flight helmet on in about 20 seconds. When I was settled in my seat next to Kenny, I plugged into the ICS and we began the start drill.

"I have the controls," I said, slipping my hands onto the collective and cyclic sticks. Kenny reached up for the starter switch of the number-one engine.

"Clear on one!" Kenny called to Bringloe from her position on the ground next to the APU.

She cleared us to proceed and we rapidly ran the sequence. It was a familiar routine and we mumbled through it at a pace that only a Hawkdriver could follow. "Number-one engine starter caution appears, master caution reset, N-G is on the rise, starter's engaged, stays engaged, T-G-T below eighty, going to idle, starting time..." The engine began to rumble to life as multiple radios transmitted frantic information while Bringloe and Capps continued to watch outside for any problems during the start.

"Got a good rise in engine oil pressure, T-G-T, RPM one and R within forty-five seconds, starter dropped out at fifty-five, T-G-T peaked at seven hundred, that's a good start on one. Clear on two?" Kenny asked.

"Two's clear!" Capps said, keeping his eyes glued to our intake and exhaust ports for any sign of fire. We repeated the sequence and brought both engines up to power. We were now RedCon 1, readiness condition one, ready to fly and fight as required. Across from us in the second Blackhawk, Captain Wilson and Alex Langa reported ready also. Now it was time for everyone to take a deep breath and focus.

"Dustoff 7-3 is RedCon 1." I keyed the transmit switch on my cyclic and went into my best impression of your bog-standard airline pilot voice. I made it a habit to keep my voice under control and upbeat. How I sounded on the radio had a trickle-down effect on my crew. At times like this, getting ready to launch into a potentially dangerous situation with lives on the line, we were all on edge. One of my biggest jobs as pilot-in-command was to keep things controlled and focus that energy. The PC always set the tone for the crew.

Captain Wilson lifted first and we yawed into position about 30 feet to his right as we turned in the direction that would lead us to the medevac. Sergeant Reyes called over the radio as we reported airborne and on the way. "Dustoff 7-2 and 7-3 in flight. I have you off at this time. Be safe, guys."

We flew as fast as we could up the valley. To our left, we spotted FOB Wright, another base supporting Operation *Hammer Down*. It was located near the village of Asadabad, or A'bad, a dot on our maps just south of the Pech River Valley. A'bad had a FARP, a Forward Arming and Refueling Point, as well as a FST, or Forward Area Surgical Team, the modern equivalent of a MASH unit from Korean War days. The FST's job was to stabilize the patients until they could be transferred to the much larger Heathe Craig Hospital in Bagram. That facility had been named for one of our old medics who had fallen to his death with a patient on a hoist mission gone bad, just a few miles from the Watapur. I had a buddy back at the FST, Captain Lall, who would be advising the staff there about Dustoff's capabilities. The only other aircraft sharing the sky near A'Bad with us that morning was a pair of OH-58D Kiowa scout helicopters just lifting from the FARP as we chugged north toward our patient.

When we had our objective area in sight, Wilson gave us his plan over the radio. "I'm gonna approach from the north. We'll have you guys hold on the ridge-line while we ingress, how copy?"

"Copy all…" I peeled out of formation to the left and pulled back on the cyclic, trading airspeed for altitude in order to climb using less power and less fuel. I could see Wilson and Langa in Dustoff 7-2 circling back toward the south and searching for a VS-17 panel on the ground that would mark the spot where the casualty waited. I glanced down at my compass and saw the white diamond indicator that showed where the GPS thought the soldiers should be. It looked like 7-2 was right on the money. As we drilled through the morning air, our headsets were full of ground radio chatter. We couldn't see much detail, but it sounded like something bad was happening on the slope below us. Platoon leaders were frantically trying get things organized and hit back at the enemy that had ambushed them. They were trying to cross a gulch and head down the other side of the mountain while Wilson and Langa were overhead, looking for the right spot to hover and pick up their wounded.

It was hard listening to the battle from a relatively safe altitude but we were all paying attention, trying to get a remote feel for what the soldiers on the ground were facing. The infantry units were having trouble determining their positions in relation to each other. They wanted air support, but they needed to know exactly where to call it in. The Taliban fighters were apparently popping up all over in a network of caves and tunnels. Bravo Company's first platoon was getting the short end of the stick. They had multiple wounded and were being flanked by an enemy force on their left. We stared down at the ground, trying to visualize what we were hearing.

"Be advised—we can light up that position but its danger-close to your people, how copy?" Circling over the fight, flights of Apaches and Kiowas were standing by to expend ordnance on the enemy but they were worried about friendly fire casualties.

"Understand that, Joker 4-3. Stand by!" The ground commander wanted to check on his maneuvering units before calling in the air. "Break, break…Gundog 2-6, Prodigal 1-6, where are you right now?"

A panting voice responded from the wayward infantry unit. "To the north of your position. We're in the far side cut at X-ray Delta 9-4-2-0-7-6-9-9. How copy?"

"Roger, understand. You move to my position. We will mass force and link up with first platoon." On the ground, a young lieutenant scrambled to the top of an exposed outcropping, trying to get a better signal to call in Dustoff for his troops. As he keyed the mike, a bullet pierced his throat, silencing him in a sudden cloud of blood. He collapsed instantly.

"Break, break…Prodigal 6 this is Prodigal 1-7. Be advised Prodigal 1-6 is KIA and I have multiple wounded."

"Prodigal 1-7, this is Prodigal 6. Understand. We have Medevac on station and close to your position."

"Negative, Prodigal 6! Hold on Dustoff! We are under concentrated RPG and small-arms fire at this time. I need gun support at previously established coordinates!"

"Prodigal 6 this is Joker 4-3. I copy all. We'll be pushing on this freq to support your Prodigal 1-7 element."

The ground unit with the call sign Prodigal 1-7 had at least one dead man—their commander—and several wounded on the ground. The Apache flight, call sign Joker 4-3, was standing by for clearance to fire in support from the air. It wasn't hard for me to follow. I'd long since learned to monitor several simultaneous radio transmissions. To this day I can listen to several conversations going on around me and follow them all. It goes with the territory in Army Aviation.

We were about to get busy, so I told Bringloe and Capps to get ready for action. Wilson and Langa in 7-2 called us on our other FM over the family internal frequency. There was no word as they reported airborne and on station about the status of their initial patient. Kenny nudged me and pointed out his window. We could see Dustoff 7-2 climbing to join up on us. I keyed my radio to let Wilson know where we were.

"I see you on my right, 7-2. Be advised we were listening to the Air Battle Net and the ground guys have multiple casualties, but we can't get in while the Apaches are working to suppress. LZ is max hot down there."

"Copy that, we heard the same from the Prodigal unit" Alex Langa said in a calm voice. "Cammack stayed on the ground to survey the situation. He's reporting the casualty is stable, but they're in a firefight. He waved us off until he could get the patient stabilized." Staff Sergeant Cammack was doing a very brave thing by staying behind and sending his aircraft out of the area so it wouldn't become an easy target for enemy gunners.

"Cammack is on the ground," I said to Kenny. "This is starting to get a little crazy." We drilled holes above the battlefield along a high ridgeline to the east for a long time, following the action on the radio and waiting for the call to head in and pick up the wounded. There was not much else for us to do except hope Cammack was OK and watch the tracers fly back and forth. The radio told us Taliban fighters were crawling out of caves all over the area and the Apache gunships had their hands full engaging multiple targets. An hour after the fight started, we spotted an Air Force F-15E Strike Eagle rocketing up the valley below us, streaming contrails from its wingtips as the pilot pulled up over the fight. The Strike Eagle made a long looping turn and came back on a bombing run to drop a JDAM or Joint Direct-Attack Munition—a smart bomb fitted with a precision guidance kit—on the enemy positions. That high-explosive package helped the situation on the ground significantly.

After the Air Force zoomed off station, the Apaches maneuvered in to add rocket and gunfire to the suppression, and it looked like Wilson and Langa might be able to get back down and pick up their patient and flight medic. It wasn't long after the air strikes that we heard from Cammack on our unit frequency. He sounded calm and unflustered despite what he had seen going on around him down on the ground.

"Dustoff 7-2, this is 7-2 Delta. Ready for pick up."

"Roger, copy; we are inbound now." We watched Wilson and Langa off to our left front aim their Blackhawk back into the valley. It was a hoist situation and we circled nearby as Cammack and his patient were lifted into the hovering aircraft. The trees on the mountainside looked wavy and distorted through the heat of 7-2's exhaust. The fight down there was not over as indicated by the crisscross pattern of tracers that laced around the aircraft.

With flight medic and patient aboard, Wilson lifted and turned for a quick trip back to FOB Wright and the FST at A'bad. They would join up on us as soon as they offloaded the wounded man, but for now, it was our turn on the rollercoaster. As we orbited high, we got fresh information from Johnny Reyes back at FOB Joyce.

"Dustoff 7-2 and 7-3, we have updates on your mission. There are two more, priority, near your last pick-up. How copy?" Wilson and Langa were halfway to FOB Wright by this time, but they responded for our flight. "Dustoff Ops, we copy your last. Send the nine-line."

At that point, things began to slide from routine to semi-serious in a hurry. Reyes interrupted himself with an update on his update. "Stand by on that last transmission. We now have two more patients, both priority—gunshot and shrapnel wounds to the hand and thigh. Prepare to copy grid…"

"Send it!" And we all started to punch GPS buttons.

"Your grid is X-ray Delta 9-3-5-2-7-6-8-4. Freq is 3-5 point 0. Contact Prodigal 1-7."

It was a familiar spot. We'd been flying over it all morning and the call sign was one of the units we heard getting chewed up in the earlier firefight. The spot for the pick-up was fairly near where we were orbiting, and Kenny thought he could see it on the ground from his side. I pulled out of the orbit and headed for the ground in a long, slow approach, looking for the VS-17 panel amid the steep, rocky terrain off our nose. It was another one of those skinny, confined ridgelines that made it tough for a pilot to decide on the safest relationship between the topography and his tail rotor.

As we searched for activity, I glanced quickly over at Kenny. He was sitting there like Yoda, his eyes masked by his tinted helmet visor. We might be heading into chaos, but Kenny Brodhead was not letting that shake him. I saw a grin forming underneath his thick yet in-regulation mustache. Many a Sergeant Major wanted to shave it off his face, but none were brave enough to murmur a word to Kenny Brodhead. With the helmet and visor, I thought he looked like a cross between Darth Vader and the little Scrubbing Bubbles icon.

Kenny keyed the ICS and told Bringloe and Capps that we were headed in to pick up two priorities, one leg wound and one hit in the wrist. "There's more down there," he said, "but 7-2 can pick them up when they get back from A'bad. Capps, this is gonna be a hoist, so get set for it."

In the back of Dustoff 7-3, Specialist David Capps went wide-eyed for a moment. He was about to get his first and second combat hoists in an area where the bad guys and the good guys were still trading fire. He took a quick look at Julia Bringloe who was busy getting her harness and medical kit ready, and then he swung the hoist out into the air rushing by the aircraft. He went over his mental checklist and then pulled on the heavy welder's glove that would protect his hand as he nursed the hoist line up and down. He grabbed the remote control and stared at it for a moment as the pilot slowed the aircraft over the soldiers waiting on the ground with the wounded men. "Ready in back," he said in what he hoped was a strong, confident tone.

"It's all you, Capps," he heard from the cockpit. "You've got power to the hoist."

Capps and Bringloe went into action. The meat of the mission was now in their hands.

"We're moving about the cabin," Capps said as he and Bringloe confirmed that they were ready. "Buddy checks complete."

Julia Bringloe moved over near Capps where she could mount the JP when the time came for descent and gave his shoulder a squeeze. "We got this, Capps."

We spotted the smoke near a stand of tall trees that were bending in our rotor wash as we approached the pick-up site. "Prodigal 1-7, Dustoff 7-3 is on short final for patient pickup. I have your smoke in sight." Kenny took the controls and settled the Blackhawk into a high hover to keep us clear of two spiky trees waving just outside my window. The key was to hold us steady against wind gusts or any other disruption and keep our rotors from becoming wood-chippers while the crew in back did their thing. It was about all we could do to help at this point. The rest was up to our crew chief and flight medic.

Capps reported that Bringloe was on the JP and he was lowering her to the ground. His voice sounded a little squeaky but fairly confident as he lowered our medic. The pickup site was peppered with obstacles like large boulders, rocky ledges, and a tall hedge of prickly bushes. There were probably worse places from which to pick up a wounded soldier, but this one was bad enough. In the cockpit we focused on holding hover and hoped it was all going well back in the cabin. It was too long since we'd heard a report from Capps. I didn't want bug him—but I did.

"Talk to me, Capps…"

Specialist David Capps was too focused to hear the request for a progress report from the cockpit. He was watching Julia Bringloe below him on the hoist line. While the pilots fought the up and down motion of the aircraft trying to hold it steady, the yo-yo motion just increased Julia's spin. And the more Capps tried to stabilize the cable, the faster Bringloe seemed to whirl. It was a bad area down there, and the soldiers who might help him were all spread out under cover. He pawed at the sweat stinging his eyes and tried to focus on getting the hoist cable under control.

"Capps, you need to talk to us right now and let us know what's going on, brother." I knew Caps was too fixated on making the hoist perfect to send progress reports, but Kenny and I were getting worried. What should be a routine hoist—even for a first-timer—was taking way too long. Capps didn't respond, but SGT Bringloe did. The rotors were creating incredible amounts of static electricity, and as Julia brushed against a tree branch, she received a painful shock. It happened several times, all the way down into a waiting thicket of thorn bushes. Now Julia was not only in pain—she was furious. She grabbed her radio and keyed the mike.

"Just put me down, Capps!"

"Trying…" We finally heard Capps' voice and he was clearly under a strain. We looked at the hillside and saw there were a couple of soldiers a few meters above the site where Julia should land.

"Just set her down, Capps." I mustered my airline pilot voice and tried to sound reassuring. "Don't keep her buddies waiting."

"Medic's on the ground," Capps finally reported and there was a perceptive tone of relief in his voice. Part one was done. Now he just had to get her and the patients back up into the aircraft.

⤫

On the ground, fighting the rotor wash of Dustoff 7-3, SGT Julia Bringloe fought clear of the Jungle Penetrator and tried to clear her head. She was flat on her back and dizzy from all the spinning on the descent and the Blackhawk above her seemed to pitch up and down which made the vertigo worse. *I'm gonna kill that kid*, she thought.

⤫

She staggered over to where the casualties were staged and took a look at their wounds. The man with the leg wound looked slightly worse. He had a tourniquet tied on by the ground medic and most of the bleeding had stopped. The other wounded man with a round through his hand would be less trouble on the lift. She unrolled the portable stretcher—called a SKED for the company that made the Army's portable rescue apparatus—and began strapping the leg-wound into it.

"We'll take him first," Julia told the ground medic. "The other guy can ride up on the hoist with me." Then she looked up at the Blackhawk still hovering overhead and keyed her radio. "Dustoff 7-3, this is 7-3 Delta on the ground. Stand by on the hoist. I'll call when we're ready."

I acknowledged her message and then talked to Capps. He needed to do better on the ascent than he had on the drop. "Capps, you got the JP, brother?"

"Yep," he said. The hoist cable and hook were back in the aircraft and Capps sounded terse and confident so I decided not to add anything at that point. Kenny pulled the aircraft off the zone to pick up a racetrack pattern above the site

until Julia called ready for hoist. We didn't wander too far
from a quick return, because it was clear that the guys on the
ground had enemy on all sides and another fight could break
out anytime. I didn't want Bringloe on the ground if that happened.

There was time for another little prayer so I said one.
*Dear God, I know I'm going to heaven when I die. I'm just
asking you to make it some other day.*

Craning back over my headrest, I could see Capps still
staring at the ground. If he was fixated on the troublesome
descent he would be no good for the trip in the other direction. "Hey, Capps, you good back there?"

Capps got on the ICS and told us he was fine. He also
launched into a long-winded explanation of what happened
on the hoist descent. We listened while we circled waiting
for our call and Kenny talked to him like a favorite uncle.
"Capps," he said in a reassuring tone, "you've got to talk to
all of us as a crew. You're our only eyes back there, man."

Capps tried to shake the nerves that were jangling through
his system. He appreciated what the pilots told him and he
vowed to do better. Meanwhile, he had managed at least a
part of his first combat hoist. It wasn't a spectacular, textbook operation but he got Bringloe on the ground safely and
he was going to get her and the wounded guys back up in the
same way—only better. He pulled his legs inside the Blackhawk and rolled the cabin door shut. He could analyze his
initial performance later, find out what he did wrong—and
correct it. But there was still a medevac mission to complete
and he knew he was a crucial part of that.

"Dustoff 7-3, 7-3 Delta is ready for pick-up at this time."

Julia sounded strong and confident on the ground and we heard no gunfire in the background, so Kenny adjusted on the controls and rolled us back toward the site. I took over on the final approach and nestled us in as tight as I could near those bothersome trees, hoping we'd shorten the time on the hoist during the ascent. Bringloe shouted instructions to the soldiers helping her on the ground. She sounded like a drill sergeant and the soldiers responded quickly to her direction. We powered up the hoist and Capps swung it out ready to drop it to her for the first casualty lift.

On the ground below Dustoff 7-3, SGT Julia Bringloe was finished loading her first patient into the SKED. She double-checked the straps and muscled the man off the ground a bit to see that the balance was stable enough to keep him from tilting too much forward or back while he rode the hoist up to the helicopter. This was a one-man operation, and it was all up to Capps once she had the man hooked up. She needed to stay with the other patient, so her crew chief was going to have to bring the man up, unhook him inside the aircraft, and then send the hoist back down for her and the man with the hand wound.

Infantry troopers who had been through the medevac drill before manhandled the hook over to Bringloe. She shifted it clear of the surrounding trees and then attached the SKED's lift straps to a D-ring, hooking it all up to the cable. When it was all secure, she reached for the tag-line at the foot end of the SKED and gave it some slack. When Capps tightened up for the lift, the casualty was bound to swing and Bringloe would check that by holding onto the line. She

called Capps to begin the lift and then watched carefully as
the stretcher began to rise off the ground.

"OK. Patient is off the ground." Capps was trying to give us
the required progress reports and focus on operating the lift.

"Very cool, man." I used my airline pilot voice, trying to
sound light and unconcerned while Capps worked in the
cabin behind us. Pilots like Kenny and I understood how important our crew-dogs were to a successful mission. We
might be controlling the aircraft, but they were doing all the
heavy lifting—literally. We left him to it and scanned the
hillsides for any sign of enemy activity.

"Patient is slowly moving to the hoist; cabling up."

"Cabling up," I confirmed. This was better. Capps was
communicating like a solid team member, and I could hear
more confidence in his voice. It seemed to be going
smoothly, but that's always when Murphy jumps up to re-
mind helicopter crews that his law is absolute and nothing
goes as planned.

Bringloe was having a tough time with the tag-line on
the ground that she was using to help control the casualty's
ascent. The load was heavy and bulky and the SKED wanted
to swing below the helicopter like a pendulum. She squatted
and pulled hard, trying to keep the load under control. The
tag-line burned through her smoking flight gloves and blis-
tered her hands. She held on despite the pain until the line
finally snapped under the strain. We couldn't see any of that
from the cockpit. We found out all was not well when Capps
came up on the ICS.

"Uh oh…" he mumbled.

"That's not what I need to hear, Capps. What's up back
there?"

"The tag line snapped! The patient is spinning!"

There was nothing we could do up in the cockpit to help. Capps reported he could probably get the spinning casualty up safely. I craned around to see him on the controls, using his feet to put friction on the hoist line until the poor guy in the stretcher was within reach. Then he muscled the man into the cabin and turned his attention to the hoist. Capps was the crew chief and mechanical stuff was his responsibility. We held the hover over the evacuation site waiting impatiently for his report.

"We've got a problem," Capps finally said. "I think the hoist is damaged." There was more. Capps thought the rubber shock-bumper above the hook was loose. He was afraid the cable might have kinked when the tag-line broke. A kinked cable could easily unwind under tension or snap under the load of a casualty or a flight medic, what was called *birdcaging*. If a hoist cable were to snap, the medic, patient or both would fall to their death. It was not a good report and we were forced to rely on Capp's judgment. If we flew off with just the one wounded soldier aboard, we'd be forced to leave Julia on the ground.

As usual, it was still the PC's call. The risk was too great. The smart move was to fly our wounded guy back to A'bad and have our hoist checked or repaired. Dustoff 7-2 was back from their first trip and conducting another hoist somewhere off to our east. They could pick up Julia and her last patient. I called Captain Wilson and quickly briefed him on our status. He said he'd recover our medic and the wounded man while we pulled off and waited for them to arrive. We didn't know if we were still in the fight or out of it. Julia watched as her boys started to climb away from her.

We loitered while CPT Wilson and Alex Langa arrived to pick up Bringloe and her patient. Once everyone was safely off the ground, we joined up and burned for A'bad at best speed. The patient wrapped in the SKED was moaning in pain, asking Capps for water and painkillers. He provided some of the former but he didn't have any of the latter. That kind of thing was flight medic territory.

"This guy is asking for morphine," Capps said. Kenny looked over his headrest and tried to see what was happening in the back. "You've had combat lifesaver training, Capps. What do you think?"

"I think if he was a jet engine I might be able to fix him." Capps was back in the game.

"He'll be fine," I said. "We'll be at A'bad in a second. Just tell him to hang on."

"Yeah—but he says he's his unit's medic."

Kenny and I exchanged a look as we made our approach to the FST landing zone. Things were rapidly going from bad to worse. We might have a damaged hoist flying medevac in an area that always required casualty hoists and now we were carrying the medic from the infantry unit that was taking the most casualties.

We filled in Wilson and Langa concerning our hoist status on the flight back to A'bad. As soon as both Blackhawks were on the ground, Alex and SGT Vaughn, the senior crew chief, jumped out and came over to help us assess the situation. We kept our bird in ground idle while they gathered around Capps to take a close look at the hoist.

I could see them scrambling around outside the cabin, grabbing at pieces of the hoist and pulling on the cable. As our maintenance officer, Alex would have the last word on whether or not our equipment was good enough to get on with the mission. He conferred briefly with Vaughn and then turned to Capps. "You think that's bad? Negative, it's not bad. It's fine. You're good to go; just calm down a little bit. You're gonna be fine."

Langa hustled up to my side of the cockpit and let me know we were back in action and fit to fly. Vaughn just slapped Capps on the helmet and smiled. "You did good, man. You finally got your first combat hoist…or at least part of one." Vaughn followed Langa back toward Dustoff 7-2 and they climbed back into their helicopter. There was a lot of work yet to be done back in the mountains. We idled for a while until Cammack and Bringloe got their patients safely in the hands of the FST medics and then came running back to remount.

As we waited to return to the battleground, I was worried that Capps might be back there second-guessing himself. That wouldn't do for the missions ahead of us. "Listen, Capps, you did the right thing. 7-2 covered it and that's the reason we're not out here alone, right? Nobody can handle situations like that all alone. You made the right call. Don't worry about it."

"Dustoff 7-2, is RedCon 1. Off in five…"

I counted five seconds and got us back in the game by pulling on the cyclic, lifting the collective and easing in a little left pedal. Takeoff in a Blackhawk seems counter-intuitive. The main rotors are turning in a horizontal plane and the tail rotor is spinning in a vertical plane. You've got to manage the cyclic and apply left tail rotor pedal a bit to counteract the torque and keep the fuselage from just spinning around under the main rotors. Stuck-wing pilots claim that a rotary-wing aircraft doesn't really fly, as much as it beats the air into submission.

We joined up on Wilson and Langa in 7-2, brought our nose down to gain speed, and headed through gathering gloom back into the valley. There were more wounded soldiers on the ground out there, and we were in for a long stretch of flying to rescue them. The radios told us the fight was intermittent but violent in a number of locations. The operation was not going as well as expected and that made everyone tense. We weren't down there facing the incoming fire, but we were soldiers and we felt for the guys who were. We would have to adapt and improvise some more before our part of Operation *Hammer Down* was finished.

CHAPTER 6: WINGMAN

Of all my accomplishments I may have achieved during the war, I am proudest of the fact that I never lost a wingman.
—Colonel Erich Hartmann

25 June 2011

WE MADE A FEW more routine pick-ups in the afternoon before we ran out of fuel and flight time. When we finally returned to FOB Joyce, everyone was tired and worried about the weather. In our little improvised ops center, Johnny Reyes pointed at one of his computer screens and shook his head. "Weather is getting worse to the southeast," he said. "And it looks like it's moving this way." If we got socked in by weather, nobody would be able to fly in and rescue the wounded.

"How is it at JAF?" I slumped onto a couch where Bringloe and Capps were filling out after-action reports.

"Still pretty good down there," Reyes reported. "Rachel Hall and Dave Fish have flown a couple of missions, dodged an RPG this morning, but other than that nothing too crazy." There was food available in the mess hall, but nobody seemed anxious to walk over and eat. If we did that, we'd likely just be interrupted in mid-meal to come sprinting back and launch on a mission. Medevac missions come when you're otherwise occupied eating, showering, or sitting on the throne in a port-a-john.

We found a box of meals wrapped in plastic trays, the little prepared rations for night-shift workers and flight crews on alert that everyone called Jimmy Deans for some long-lost reason. We lounged around picking at cold ravioli and fruit cups, listening to the action up in the mountains on the tactical nets. Captain Wilson translated and did the play-by-play as we tried to follow what was happening in the fight farther up in the Watapur Valley.

"They're gonna try to reinforce that cut-off platoon tonight," Wilson said around a mouthful of fruit cocktail. "There's a village up there in the mountains near the bad guys' training camp. The whole operation is stuck until they can get into that village. It's a typical deal. They've got AQ and Talibs shooting at them all over the area, and the locals in the village are caught in the middle of it all."

Over in the surgical area, we could see the wounded ground medic we'd evacuated earlier stumping around on a crutch. He was complaining loudly about the rough ride he'd had on the hoist after Bringloe's tag-line snapped. I was sure Kenny was going to finish him off for crying like a baby and insulting his medic. Julia just rolled her eyes and went back to the cold ravioli. There were no requests for medevacs by the time we finished our reports, so we decided it might be safe to move our gear from the fly-blown tents to nicer models that were available closer to the LZ.

When we arrived at our new digs, the first thing we noticed was a blast of cool air. Some saint on the accommodations crew had gotten the AC working. This tent even featured steel bunk-beds that looked a lot more comfortable than the canvas cots we used the previous night. I picked a lower, dropped my gear, and collapsed onto a mattress in a cloud of dust. I pulled the wool horse blanket off the bed and made myself a little cocoon that would block out waning sunlight, spread out my sleeping bag and rolled into it. Everyone else followed suit in any way that worked to let them sleep and our 4th Platoon medevac section was unconscious in minutes.

"Medevac, medevac, medevac!" We were jolted awake after a couple of hours by another medevac alert. Captain Wilson and Alex Langa mustered their crew and told us to go back to sleep. They'd take the mission and let us rest up for whatever might happen that night. I tried to relax and get back to sleep after they banged their way out of the tent, but it wasn't working. I was still awake about an hour later when we heard a Blackhawk landing out on the LZ. The crew of 7-2 strolled into our tent saying they'd had no problems on the mission, but didn't provide many other details. Wilson stopped by my bed to let me know he would handle anything else that dropped during the rest of the day. Unless we got a multi-patient mission that required both birds, Wilson and Langa would fly solo until they ran out of flight time and had to take crew-rest. The captain wanted at least one crew as fresh as possible for night medevac missions. I rolled over and tried to sleep but I was just dozing fitfully by the time we got another call. The ops guys called for both crews, so we rolled out of our sacks and went to see what was in store for the final daylight hours.

Sergeant Johnny Reyes met us at the door with the nine-line for an urgent medevac up near an Afghan *qalat,* or fortified mountain village. "It's the Prodigal 1-7 guys again," he said. "We don't know how many evacs yet, but the LZ will definitely be hot."

"Same outfit," I said grabbing a piece of paper to copy the details as they came in, "the one that's been pinned down all day." The infantry unit that bore the call-sign Prodigal 1-7 was having a tough time. They had a platoon leader killed near a fortified village in a spot where we couldn't reach him due to all the incoming. Retrieving dead soldiers was something that we had to do—it was called a Hero Mission among medevac crews—but we handled it as routine. The priority was wounded men who had a chance of survival if we could get them out and back to medical treatment. The dead man would have to wait. A helicopter shot out of the sky while trying to retrieve a dead soldier would only complicate matters for the infantry.

"Let's get fired up and go…" Captain Wilson sent Langa, Cammack, and Vaughn out to his aircraft. He grabbed me by the elbow as I started to follow. "Sabby, we'll take this one. You guys go back to sleep and keep your crew fresh." Before I could say anything he was gone out the door shouting at Reyes to feed him the rest of the pertinent info after they were airborne.

Orders are orders but I didn't like this one. What if there were more casualties than 7-2 could handle? What if something went wrong with them like it did with us earlier in the day? I paced around the area for a while, deciding to forego further efforts at sleep. This whole deal didn't feel right, and when Wilson and Langa reported on station over the battlefield, I found out why. There was a huge firefight going on around that *qalat* where the wounded were waiting. Flights of Apaches and Kiowas had been buzzing around it for hours trying to suppress the enemy fire, but it wasn't working as scripted. The bad guys were firmly dug in and resisting all attempts to push or blast them out of their fortified position. Wilson reported he was punching holes in the sky, waiting for clearance to head in and pick up the casualties.

We were about to go back to the tent when Reyes shouted an update. "Sir, they are now reporting three urgents total!"

That was going to be more than 7-2 could handle, and urgent meant there was no time to fool around with multiple lifts.

"Call second-up crew—right now!" I shouted and headed out the door. I hopped into 9-4-4 and powered up the systems. Kenny Brodhead was right behind me and hopped in just as I hit the starter for the number one engine. Bringloe and Capps slammed their gear into Dustoff 7-3 and helped us short-cut the start procedures. We were turning blades and airborne in four minutes flat.

We were roaring toward the mouth of the Watapur Valley when I finally remembered to check in with ops. "Dustoff 7-3 is airborne enroute to assist 7-2 at this time."

"Copy that, 7-3." Reyes gave us a place to look for Wilson and Langa. "Be advised 7-2 is holding to the east and waiting for clearance to go in."

We pumped on the speed, giving the Blackhawk more collective, forcing more fuel into the engines and pitching the blades at best angle to climb quickly toward the mountains. Dustoff 7-2 was still running around in a holding pattern when we joined up on them. I could see Staff Sergeant Vaughn in back prepping his hoist, but we still had not gotten clearance from the grunts to come in and pick up the wounded men. It was late afternoon with shadows lengthening all across the valley, there were soldiers in need of urgent rescue on the ground, and the firefight around the village was still raging. I prayed that the ground medics could keep those guys alive until we had a chance to get them.

Wilson's voice revealed his frustration when he called us with a plan. "We'll take the first two patients," he said. "You guys can follow and get any others—if we ever get a chance to get in there."

We choppered around the peaks for about a half-hour, listening to frantic voices on the ground frequency and watching tracers fly across the area. Kenny checked his watch and pointed at the sun sinking toward the peaks to the west. "We're gonna run out of time waiting around like this, Erik."

"Yeah, we're gonna need some help up here pretty soon. At this rate both of our crews will run out of duty day before sunset." In normal situations, the Army sets strict limits on the amount of time pilots and aircrew are allowed to fly without adequate rest. It sometimes gets cheated in emergencies, but every aviator wants to be rested and at his best. Too many accidents, losses, injuries, and deaths were due to exhausted flight crews.

Captain Wilson in Dustoff 7-2 was thinking along the same lines. "Dustoff 7-3…7-2. Listen, you guys are better off heading back to Joyce until we can get cleared in on this thing. We're running out of time and options."

"Agreed…" I told him with a sinking feeling that we were somehow abandoning fellow soldiers in need on the battlefield. If we ran out of regulation flying time, we'd either have to bend the rules and risk accidents or misjudgments or we'd have to pass missions along to some other outfit. There was an element of pride involved, and no one wanted to pass on a mission for any reason. Alex and CPT Wilson were a good cockpit, but I still prayed for them. "We'll go back and try to save some duty time. Call if the LZ calms down."

We made it back to FOB Joyce in ten minutes with plenty of fuel still onboard. We shut down and ambled into the aid station. Nobody was going anywhere. The call to get back out there could come anytime. We milled around aimlessly listening to the radios and talking to the ops guys for about a half-hour, and then the report came that the medevac LZ was finally clear of hostile fire. We scrambled back out to the Blackhawk, got it cranked, and lifted off in the late afternoon heat.

When we arrived over the area, we let 7-2 know we were standing by. Wilson and Langa were already plummeting down toward the medevac site. Alex was flying and pouring on the speed, snaking down a ridgeline to the north, then snap-turning to the left just over the disputed *qalat*. He'd been shot up at least once too often, so he was giving enemy gunners down there as small and elusive a target as possible. There were a couple of Kiowas hanging around to support 7-2 if they caught ground fire. Alex hauled the Blackhawk into an aerial wheelie, yanking the nose up and coming to a hover right over a mud hut.

Up in 7-3 we were admiring the approach when things got hot in a hurry. Just as 7-2 settled into a stable configuration, we saw an RPG streak through the gloom. It missed their main rotor by less than a foot. Kenny pointed at a flash just above them as the rocket round impacted on the hillside showering 7-2 and everyone on the LZ with shrapnel and rock shards. We rolled around trying to spot the shooters as the Kiowas thundered into the area trying to do the same. There was a blaze of muzzle-flash below and we saw rounds stitch into the Blackhawk fuselage.

"Dustoff 7-2 is taking fire," Alex radioed calmly as if it wasn't obvious to everyone in the air and on the ground. As we dropped down lower, taking up a position to help or replace 7-2 if they went down, we saw the infantry open up in a wall of fire trying to suppress the enemy shooters. In the light, the tracers looked like a glowing spider web spreading all across the hillside. The fight was back on and Alex pulled pitch to get out of the way.

The ground radios were squawking with requests for information or status reports as 7-2 peeled off the LZ and clawed for altitude. I steered us close to them so that we'd be right on top of things if they fell out of the sky. Leadership training says the mission comes first, but that damaged helicopter contained some of my best friends, and we were determined to do everything we could to see that they survived. 7-2 climbed to clear the ridgeline. I ignored the ground radio net and called Wilson and Alex and to find out how much damage had been done.

"We're smelling hydraulic fluid." Alex sounded cool and collected. Kenny and I felt sick. In a helicopter, smelling hydraulic fluid can signal a lot of things—and none of them are good. If the crew smells hydraulic fluid, it means fluid is escaping from one or both systems that require hydraulic pressure to function. If they lost the number one hydraulic system, they could lose control of the tail rotor, which could put them into a spin and crash. If they lost the second system, it would be like losing the power-steering in a car. There were no parachutes in Army helicopters, so if 7-2 lost hydraulics, including the back-up system, they were bound to crash. Ground fire has a tendency to decimate vulnerable helicopter hydraulics.

They had been hit with a pretty long spray of rounds that missed Staff Sergeant Cammack by inches, Alex reported, as he and Wilson ran through check-lists to see if they could remain airborne. They had a bunch of illuminated caution lights on the dash panel and we talked emergency procedures as we pulled up into formation with them. Down below us, the Kiowa pilots were buzzing over the area like angry hornets, trying to find a target and avenge what the enemy had done to a couple of their fellow aviators.

The damaged aircraft was still climbing for altitude when Alex gave me his assessment. "Brother, I've got a number-one reservoir low-caution light, number-one hydraulic-

pump caution light and number one tail rotor servo is out..."
Kenny and I listened to his litany of woe and tried to figure
out what systems on the bird were still working. We were
approaching FOB Joyce having traded guesses and advice
by the time Alex and Wilson thought they had a handle on
how badly they were shot-up and what they might do to get
7-2 safely back on the ground.

It was not a pretty picture. Dustoff 7-2 had lost the number one hydraulic pump and likely had damage to their tail
rotor. They wouldn't know for sure until they tried to hover.
If they spun out of control, their estimate would be confirmed. Alex decided that he was going to try for a roll-on
landing at high speed. If he could pull it off, the forward momentum would hopefully keep the aircraft pointed in the
right direction until he could get the landing gear on the
ground. If he couldn't accomplish that and counteract the
main rotor torque, they would simply spin out of control.
That did not seem like a good option. 7-2 was bleeding out
fast. Alex and Wilson isolated the leak before it got worse.
The aircraft was now urgently wounded.

A high-speed roll-on landing was precisely the type of
thing Alex and I had practiced back at J'bad a couple of
weeks before we launched in support of this mission. I
thought about another helicopters truism: Plenty of practice
prevents poor performance. I said another prayer for Alex
and his crew as they passed FOB Joyce out of their left door.
A pair of Blackhawks suddenly appeared coming at us head-
to-head.

"Dustoff 7-2, this is Chill 5-4, we have you in sight." It
was a familiar voice. One of the Blackhawks joining up on
us was being flown by the senior maintenance test pilot of
our task force. He'd been flying a mission elsewhere in the
valley when he heard about the damage to Wilson and Alex's

aircraft. He made a decision to escort Dustoff 7-2 back to Jalalabad where maintenance experts could get to work on it. "Dustoff 7-3," he radioed us. "We've got your boys and we'll escort them back to JAF."

We were off the hook for a while. We were also now the only medevac helicopter available at Joyce to support the operation, and there were still wounded on the ground. We needed fuel. It would have to be a hot-refuel without shutting down. We needed to get back in the fight. I called the FARP and alerted them we were coming in for quick juice-up and would be departing soonest thereafter.

"Better just get the minimum we'll need," Kenny recommended. "That'll keep us light and we can always come back for more."

As we hovered into the FARP to get fuel, I thought about Julia Bringloe in the back. She hadn't said a word during the crisis with 7-2. As we landed and she and Capps went through the drill to let us know we were ready to take on fuel, I listened closely to her voice. There was an edge of tension in it. She had to be thinking about what lay ahead after we got gas and launched back into the valley. As the fueling soldier dragged the six-inch hoses to our left and plugged in to our aircraft to begin pumping jet fuel, she leaned against the gunner's window, watching the fuel crew while chomping on a handful of gummy-bears. She knew where we were going when we lifted off again and it had to be working on her mind that she was now the only flight medic available this far east in Afghanistan.

In a few minutes, the fuel gauge told me we had picked up 1,200 pounds, and that was enough if we intended to stay light. "Cut 'em off, Julia," I said. She gave a hand signal to the fuel crew, who disconnected the nozzle, buttoned us back up, and got out of the way.

As we lifted off from the FARP, I swallowed the tension and tried to sound cheery as I briefed everyone on what we were going to do. Kenny just smiled and nodded as I ran it down for everyone. "What we're gonna do here…" I said. "…is head back and loiter until we get cleared to go in and get the casualties. By that time, we'll be out of duty-day time, so we'll bring them back here and shut down. You know 7-2 is gonna be fine and they'll send somebody up from J'bad to give us a hand as soon as they can. Meanwhile, we're the only game in town, and those soldiers up in the valley need us. You guys ready for this?"

"Ready back here." Capps sounded confident.

"Let's do it," Bringloe said with commitment.

Kenny called us clear of the FARP and outbound for the Watapur Valley. "A'bad, don't get sleepy. We'll be back shortly with more wounded."

I lifted the aircraft and pointed the nose toward the fight in the hills. As we drove up the valley, now the closest stand-by medevac available to the guys on the ground, I tuned into the ground nets. The fight was still on up there and there were bound to be casualties. Any pick-ups we had to make on this leg of the flight would be at night. That complicated matters and the only upside was that the enemy gunners would have a harder time getting an effective bead on us.

In the cockpit of Dustoff 7-2, Alex Langa squirmed in his seat, trying to merge himself with the damaged helicopter he was flying. An experienced pilot like Langa felt the aircraft like a doctor probing for problems in the body of a sick patient. He was a human sensor, feeling for subtle changes in flight control responses, unusual vibrations, or any little indication that the bird might resist what he needed it to do.

Captain Wilson was the command pilot, but he was smart enough to let the more experienced aviator fly the emergency landing they had to make at J'bad. While Alex Langa nursed the helicopter along, Wilson sat waiting to provide any assistance his co-pilot might need. Alex thought of his wife Amy and reached up to touch Mister Moose, his newborn son Max's stuffed animal that always rode along on his helicopter dash. Wilson was thinking about his wife as well back in New York and hoped he'd get to see her again—but all that was up to the man sitting next to him.

Langa had been on the controls of 7-2 for a full 20 minutes, which seemed like seconds when the city of Jalalabad came into sight off their nose. It was now or never, and he keyed the radio to alert the tower that they were coming in for an emergency landing with two escorts in close formation.

"JAF Tower, Dustoff 7-2 is a flight of three UH-60s to the north Alpha Sector inbound. Dustoff 7-2 will be making an emergency landing to 1-3. Escorts Chalk 2 and 3 will break off and go to the FARP."

"Dustoff 7-2, roger. You're cleared to land runway 1-3. Winds are currently 1-7-0 at fifteen knots gusting to twenty. Temperature four-five, altimeter two-niner-five-two. Crash rescue is standing by…"

Langa acknowledged and stared down at the 7,000 foot runway where he'd have to execute the landing. There were fire trucks and ambulances clustered around mid-field as he slowly lost altitude, keeping the power on to generate the wind velocity that would hopefully help him keep the aircraft from spinning. He needed to constantly monitor his groundspeed, but there were a lot of other things that needed doing. He asked Wilson to keep an eye on the groundspeed indicator. "Call me below sixty…" Alex focused on the runway centerline and barely caught a glimpse of the gawkers watching for the worst and hoping for the best as he breezed by them.

"You're below sixty now—holding at fifty-nine." Wilson's voice contained none of the tension he was feeling as they flew along the runway, gradually losing altitude. In the back of the Blackhawk, Cammack, and Vaughn braced in their seats and snugged up the inertia-reel locks on their safety harnesses. Everybody noted what exit they'd use if this didn't work, and a second choice if that escape route became blocked by fire, metal—or both.

Alex Langa tightened his muscles while trying to keep a light touch on the controls. They would contact the ground momentarily—one way or the other. He lowered the collective which should put their tail wheel on the ground and chewed on his lip while he waited to see what would happen. He felt the touch of the gear and bottomed-out the collective with one hand while he kept the cyclic in a neutral position with the other. Either the Blackhawk would settle down onto the main gear or they would spin and likely flip over. He'd done everything by the book. Now it was a matter of fate and physics.

The main gear slammed into the tarmac jolting the pilots and crew, but there was no spin or other dangerous behavior as Dustoff 7-2 rolled down the runway past the crash crews and the flashing lights on the tower and rolled to a stop. There was not much to say. Alex reached up and patted the dash-panel as if to thank the Blackhawk for cooperating. Alex Langa and Drew Wilson shut it down and unstrapped from their seats. Brian Cammack and Phillip Vaughn climbed out of the back and stood looking at their shot-up ride. They were going to leave 7-2 right where it sat out there on the runway. Someone else could hook it up and drag it over to the maintenance hangar. They had had enough for one day.

Once the crew was on the ground, the tense silence finally broke. Standing in a pool of hydraulic fluid that was leaking from the aircraft, they whooped and hugged Alex Langa, thanking him for a truly magnificent job of flying in a damaged aircraft that might have killed them all. Unit mechanics and crash crewmen scrambled to hook a tow to the Blackhawk and haul it clear of the active runway. The shaky crew walked ahead of the tug into the sunset and talked amiably about the experience and the mission. They were safe and sound on the ground but Dustoff 7-3 was still out there, and all of them wanted to get back in action to support that crew. The sun was nearly down beyond the mountains and the weather was closing in all over the area. Dustoff 7-3 was in for some tough flying with no back-up out there in the sky over the Watapur Valley.

Dustoff 7-3 was still on mission, flying through a rapidly darkening sky and headed back toward the battlefield. We were the only medevac now, and I was hoping that Wilson and Langa in 7-2 managed a safe landing at J'bad. There had been no report on that as yet, but we'd get the word eventually. Meanwhile, I needed to focus. I ran a mental checklist in the same way I did when taking off or landing in a helicopter, compartmentalizing things and switching off what I couldn't afford to think about while I concentrated on night flying and waited for clearance to pick-up the wounded below us. I switched off the worry about Tess back at home, shut down concerns about the battle going on in the valley, and ignored questions about a hundred other things that had nothing to do with our current situation. The last mental switch I flipped was the one that concerned my survival. If I worried about that, if I focused on self-preservation, it would dominate and might prevent us from doing what had to be done to save those soldiers wounded in battle down below us.

We were alone on the mission now, but we were alone together, a tight crew and a solid team, and we would do whatever needed doing to save lives. There was no telling what lay in store—whatever it turned out to be, Dustoff 7-3 would have to handle it.

CHAPTER 7: TREEHUGGER

> **You haven't seen a tree until you've**
> **seen its shadow from the sky.**
> —Amelia Earhart

25 June 2011

"DUSTOFF 7-3, THIS IS OPS," Johnny Reyes called from FOB Joyce while we drilled through the night sky over the Watapur Valley. "Just letting you know that 7-2 is down and safe at JAF."

That was excellent news. Kenny and I grinned and made a few comments about what a great pilot Alex Langa was. We were going to miss him and CPT Wilson. They were the only other crew flying out of FOB Joyce and our relief when we ran out of flying time. And when CPT Wilson was absent, I became the AMC or Air Mission Commander by default. Any air support we got on a medevac mission was now my responsibility, and I didn't need the distraction. There was a serious fight going on down below us as we orbited at 11,000 feet, skirting the mountains surrounding the valley.

We alternated race-track patterns with figure-eights to avoid becoming predictable and watched an A-10 Warthog make a firing pass, hosing enemy positions with the 30mm cannon in its nose. It looked like a jungle down below on the hillsides. They were covered with tall trees that we'd have to avoid judiciously once we were cleared in to pick up the wounded. There was a flight of Kiowas orbiting below us, and I'd been talking to them regularly to get updates on the

LZ we needed. They were closer to the fight, and could see what was happening as the infantry and attack aircraft worked to suppress the enemy fire so we could get into the zone.

Kenny Brodhead was flying while I tried to watch the action below. We were in rough air, and he fought the controls trying to hold us steady. There was some serious turbulence coming off the mountains as the sun dropped and the air cooled. Darkness was beginning to creep in on us and we'd have to switch to night-vision devices before too long. I wanted to get into the zone and pick up the wounded before that happened. Tall trees, enemy fire, and darkness would complicate things significantly.

Flights of Air Force F-15s and F-16s were zooming low trying to force the enemy to crawl back in their holes. It was hard to tell if the air show was working, so I switched to the number two FM radio and called the Kiowa flight. "Horsemen 7-4, this is Dustoff 7-3. Any updates on the LZ?"

"We're still suppressing the target. Hope to have you in there soon, guys." It was a familiar voice, Captain Wesley Prichett from Jalalabad. The Kiowa drivers from our Task Force in their small, highly maneuverable birds watched over the medevac crews like big brothers, and I was always glad to have them along on a mission. When we got hit, they took it personally and usually burned up everything they had to suppress the people shooting at us. The problem they were facing right now, along with the Air Force assets supporting the infantry, was finding targets. The enemy forces were engaged with the grunts at close range, and it was hard to tell innocent civilians from menacing bad guys while in the air.

Watching the tiny sliver of sun disappearing on the western horizon, we needed to get ready for the switch to NVGs or Night Vision Goggles. It didn't look like we'd be cleared into the zone before full dark. I called Capps and had him break out the night-flying gear for us. He handed up two heads-up display monocles for me and Kenny. These were special attachments to the standard NVGs designed to allow pilots wearing goggles to still see their instrument displays as they looked out into the night. We checked the battery packs on the back of our helmets and plugged the monocles into a power outlet overhead, and then sent Capps to get NVGs for himself and Bringloe out of the equipment storage boxes in the back.

Kenny took a look at the shadows growing longer and darker on the hillsides and then checked the sun. "I think we can wait a little," he said, so we laid the monocle sets on the dashboard. Kenny loved flying with NVGs—a whole lot more than I did. He'd spent more time with goggles on his face than I had flying a Blackhawk. When we had to go to night-vision gear, one pilot at a time would put it on while the other one flew until both pilots were secure with the weird colors and limited field of view. I was about to change that and have everyone goggle up when ops called with a new mission.

"Dustoff 7-3, we have another urgent. Prepare to copy."

"Go for 7-3…."

Johnny Reyes sent us a grid and let us know it was the battered outfit called Prodigal 1-7 again. They had a man down with heat-stroke, and he'd likely die from it if we didn't go get him in a hurry. "Also be advised," Reyes said when he gave us the rest of the nine-line information, "they have a KIA on the ground. He's an ANA Terp." One of the Afghan National Army interpreters had been killed in the fight, but he would have to wait until we dealt with the heat-stroke. It was a simple matter of priorities and I made the call.

"Copy all," I said. "We'll get the live one now and come back for the hero. We're still waiting for clearance to pick up three criticals around the village."

I turned and bled off altitude, looking into the gloom for the smoke that the ground guys popped close to what we called the POI or Point Of Injury. We saw the GPS indication, and it was very near a stand of tall trees. I maneuvered us toward the safest spot to keep our tail rotor clear. In the back, Bringloe and Capps were getting ready for what was going to be a hoist mission.

"Right and left rear moving about the cabin," said Capps as we drilled in on the approach. "Buddy checks complete," he said. "Medic is on the JP." They were ready to go as soon as we got the Blackhawk into position. Kenny turned on power to the hoist and let Capps know it was ready for him to assume control.

"Cabin door is coming open—booming out." Capps was doing a much better job of communicating this time, and his voice sounded calm and collected. While he and Julia watched the trees and kept us advised on the approach, Kenny sent a situation report to the Kiowas.

"Horsemen 7-4 and 7-5, Dustoff 7-3, we're gonna knock out another mission here. We'll be right back for the guys near the village."

It got darker down among the pines on that hillside and I wished we'd gone ahead with the NVGs when we had the chance. Goggles are heavy and bulky, pushing your head down your shoulders. The field of view is small so you move your head constantly. Still, they were better than guessing about potential collisions. Looking for the spot the soldiers had selected for our pick-up, I loosened my grip on the controls and continued the descent. The lower we got, the darker it got, and by the time we were over the POI, it was harder to see any detail. The heavy cloud layer that had moved into the area over the western mountains hid much of the waning sunlight left in the day. It was officially dusk, and although Kenny was comfortable with it, to me it might as well have been midnight on that mountainside.

I was beginning to lose visual references when we spotted a plume of red smoke rising from a spot on a ridiculously steep slope. That was a smoke grenade marking the spot where the casualty waited. The entire area was spiked with hundred-foot pines and dotted with huge boulders. This was no place to be blind. I pulled it into a hover with 170 feet showing on the radar altimeter and we went to NVGs.

"I'll goggle up first," Kenny said while I held the bouncing Blackhawk in a shaky hover. While he got situated, I kept my eyes on the chin bubble below my feet, using it as a frame for the top of one of the tallest trees. I fought with the controls, trying to hold that treetop in exactly the same place in the frame. Without night vision aids, it was more like trying to keep a dark shape in the center of a darker shape. The last time I'd heard about a pilot trying a combat hoist at night without NVGs was in Vietnam. Those guys either had cat eyes or just a bunch of guts. While Kenny focused his NVGs and I tried to hold us in position, Capps lowered Julia Bringloe to the ground, spinning violently like she was riding one of the teacups at Disneyland. Julia hit the ground with a thud.

I'm really gonna kill that kid, she thought as she tried to stand and stumbled around trying to get her legs to stay under her shoulders. *This is a confidence builder.* A couple of soldiers rushed down to give her a hand. *These guys probably think the Army sent them a drunk chick as a special gift.* Kenny said he could see her sprinting uphill toward the marked spot among the trees.

"Slide right...three...two...one...hold hover." I followed directions as Capps ordered us closer to the pick-up spot. It was a difficult proposition even for minor maneuvers. I kept my eyes scanning around the instrument cluster from the vertical situation indicator to the vertical speed indicator, with an occasional glance at the chin bubble. My reference treetop was disappearing, and I needed to get my NVGs on before we continued.

"You good?" I asked Kenny.

"All set," he said and took the controls. I grabbed for my NVGs and heads-up monocle.

"Awesome." I began to see the world outside the Blackhawk in stunning shades of bright green. When I felt comfortable with the new vision perspective, I found that reference tree again and took the controls to stabilize our hover. "How's it going back there, Capps?"

"Right rear is goggled up," he responded. "Bringloe is with the patient and she's got him in a SKED."

Below the hovering helicopter and hidden among the pines, Julia Bringloe took a closer look at the heat-stroke casualty. He was severely dehydrated but responsive. There was a small clutch of his squad-mates sitting around looking worried for their buddy. He was wrapped up in a cocoon and about to get an e-ticket ride up through the trees. She was worried about the SKED getting snagged in the branches. A lot of hoist cable had been deployed, and that was asking for a tangle on the ascent. If the SKED snagged, Capps would have to cut the guy loose and the fall would kill him. On the other hand, if she forgot about the SKED and just rode up with him, she could fight through any trouble they might encounter on the lift. "This isn't gonna work," she said to one of the soldiers. "Help me get him out of this thing. I'll ride up with him on the hook."

The soldiers jumped to the job and got their buddy out of the big green burrito that encased his limp body. He was a big man, very wobbly on his feet, and easily twice her size. Julia and a couple of his buddies got him into a clear area where she could retrieve the JP and get them aboard for the lift. *Capps is on the mark*, she thought, as the Jungle Penetrator dropped right at her feet.

"Can you shine a light right here?" One of the soldiers clicked on a small flashlight and pointed it at the JP. The hook was good to go. Julia loaded her man and secured him with a safety harness. Then she hooked herself in and wrapped her arms around the man. She looked up and gave Capps a thumbs-up. When there was tension on the cable and they began to rise, she hugged the casualty tighter and tried to reassure him. "I got you," she said. "Here we go."

Staring down at the hoist load through his NVGs, Capps kept us abreast of what was happening with Julia and the casualty. "Medic and patient are on the JP. Cabling up. They're light. Medic and patient are off the ground. They're coming up slowly." I was impressed and so was Kenny as we glanced across the cockpit at each other. Capps was on the mark this time, sounding like an experienced pro. The winds were hard on us trying to hold the aircraft steady and it was also having an effect on Julia Bringloe and her patient. Capps reported they were at about 60 feet off the ground and oscillating in the breeze off the mountain.

"I'm trying to null it out," he said, struggling with his hands to keep the cable and load from swinging below the aircraft. The guy riding up was heavy, and his weight was making the pendulum swings long and severe. I looked at the treetops and tried to gauge the wind. All I could see were pines swirling in circles under our rotor wash. We couldn't be much help. It was all up to Capps and his rapidly growing skill with the hoist.

✑

Julia Bringloe, on the oscillating line with her arms wrapped around the heat-stroke casualty, was beginning to wonder if she was ever going to get a normal ride on a hoist. The patient screamed, thinking they were in more trouble than they were. "It's OK," she said to the frightened soldier. "We're gonna be fine. Just stay with me now."

They were passing through thick branches that she swatted or bent as they rose steadily, still swinging wildly from side to side and occasionally missing tree trunks. The helicopter couldn't get any lower without chopping into those trees and shattering the rotors, so it was going to be a relatively long ride. They were about 150 feet from the aircraft, engulfed in a huge thicket of pine trees. As she looked up to gauge their progress, she just missed getting brained by a spiky branch. She looked over her patient's shoulder and used a hand to shove them away. The JP began to oscillate slowly. She looked around trying to find a handhold or something that would allow her to control the spin. Now the spin was violent and very fast. They were spinning and barreling toward a 90-foot pine with thick, broken branches that looked like huge spikes that could skewer her and her patient. She twisted around to put her body in the path of the impact. If someone was going to get skewered on this hoist, Julia decided it ought to be her—and not her patient.

The impact felt like hitting a brick wall. It knocked her breathless, and she felt a sharp pain in her lower leg where it had been trapped between the steel hook and the tree. She had no penetrating wounds. Somehow she'd slid between the spikes and slammed into the tree trunk. They were steadily rising through a dust cloud raised by the impact as she tried to regain normal breathing. They'd gotten off fairly easy. It could have been much worse, and her patient was unharmed.

Capps reported what had happened, and that Julia and her patient appeared to be OK. He was continuing with the hoist and nearly had them clear of the trees. "Medic and patient are at the door," he announced at last. "Booming in…"

I confirmed his call as the large hydraulic arm rotated back toward the cabin. Capps scrambled away from the door to make room for Julia and her patient. When they were within reach, he helped her get the guy into the helicopter as she was clearly in pain from her ordeal on the hoist line. Then he slammed the cabin door shut and told me to pull pitch to get us out of there. I pulled us up and away from the trees. Both Kenny and I were sore and tense from holding the hover in rough air surrounded by big trees for a long, dangerous combat hoist mission. Now we could do a little more relaxed flying while we rushed the heat-stroked soldier back to the FST at A'bad.

Kenny got on the radios to let everyone know what their medevac support was doing. "Prodigal 1-7, we have your wounded. We'll be back in a few minutes."

Ten minutes later, we were approaching the LZ at FOB Wright when Capps came up on the ICS. "Medic says the patient is OK—just a little shook from the rough ride." There was a long pause. "I think she's hurt worse than he is."

When we landed, I intended to check on her, but Bringloe was already leaning into the big soldier and helping him toward the FST. She was limping on her damaged leg, and I wondered if she'd have to stay in the FST with her patient for treatment. We'd know in a little while. I called Capps back into the aircraft and we hovered 9-4-4 over to the FARP for some fuel.

Two ground medics met Julia and her patient as they staggered into the FST. One of them reached for Julia and tried to support her. "I'm not hurt," she said brushing him back and pointing at the hulking man leaning on her shoulder. "He is." While the medics hustled her patient away for treatment, she pulled off her helmet and limped over to a sink where she could roll up the leg of her flight suit to get a look at the damage. There was some blood from a gash where she'd barked her shin up against the tree and the whole lower leg was swollen and turning an ugly purple. It hurt, but she was fairly sure nothing was broken. She was likely to see some soldiers hurt a lot worse before the night ended. After washing the wound under a spray of water, she jammed her helmet back on and limped for the door.

After taking on fuel, I lifted Dustoff 7-3 and slid back toward the FST landing pad, making room for a gaggle of attack and scout birds that needed to refuel or rearm. When we settled onto the pad, I looked over and saw Bringloe limping toward us. She plugged back into the ICS. I asked how she was doing, listening carefully to her tone when she responded. She was the kind of soldier that would fight through pain, but I needed to be sure she was capable of helping us on the mission.

"You OK?"

"I'm fine." She sounded casual and unconcerned.

"You're limping pretty badly. You want to quit?" I said, smiling.

"Negative. I'm good. Let's get out of here."

We lifted off into a starless night wearing our NVGs. It was true dark, an ebony pit, with none of the ambient light you see flying over cities and towns in most other parts of the world. I struggled through the air, my NVGs dimming down for lack of ambient light. It was like swimming through ink, and we backed ourselves up with the instrumentation until we hooked off the main route and into the Watapur Valley. We quickly spotted the strobe lights of a number of helicopters racing around the area. On a hillside to our front, tracers arced up and down between two sides of a firefight. The entire east side of the valley looked like it was covered with a blanket of fireflies.

In the back, we could hear Bringloe and Capps discussing the brutal hoist mission. She was happy with his progress in controlling the load and anxious to assure him that her getting banged up wasn't his fault. "Sir, are we gonna keep this up all night?" Capps asked, aware of how much time we were all spending in the air. The clock on our duty day was ticking.

"Captain Wilson says he's trying to get O'Brien's crew up here to give us a hand before the weather closes them in back at J'bad." That was as much of an answer as I really needed to give. Our crew would fly as long as we had to if necessary, but Kenny and I believed in sharing any and all information we had. "If they get weathered in, we're gonna be cut off for a while. Pretty much the whole eastern part of the country is socked in right now. We might not get another bird. The Air Force has a CASEVAC bird at JAF, but if they send it up to us, we will end up with only our one spare to cover the whole J'bad area. If that goes down, we're done.

No medevacs for anybody. Besides, Pedro can't fly as high as we can anyway. They're doing what they can."

"So, in other words," Capps said, "we got the mission, now get on with it, right?"

"Yep. We're not leaving wounded men on the ground as long as we can fly."

"And they've got some more infantry inserts inbound on Chinooks," Kenny added. "You know what that means. Don't go to sleep back there."

CHAPTER 8: DANGER CLOSE

When I have Your Wounded.
—The last words of "Mr. Dustoff", MAJ Charles L. Kelly

25 June 2011

"DUSTOFF 7-3, THIS IS JOKER 2-6 flight of two. We're currently west of the Prodigal 1-7 element providing suppressive fire with the Horsemen for your ingress. You are cleared to the LZ now."

The Apache drivers and the Kiowa gunships were doing what they could to suppress the bad guys blazing away at the infantry on the ground. It was a welcome call. We'd been orbiting for what seemed like hours over the Watapur battlefield, waiting until we had some chance of picking up the wounded without getting blown out of the air. Waiting is always the worst part of the medevac mission, but there's never any sense calling us into a site where enemy fire is so heavy that we lose a helicopter and crew. You can't save anybody if you're sitting dead in the middle of a smoking wreck.

The infantry was also anxious for us to get going. They'd been waiting as long as we had, trying to keep the wounded alive and stable until we could get to them. "I guess it's about as clear as it's gonna get," I said to the crew.

"Let's just get in there," Kenny said. "Those guys have waited long enough."

"You guys OK with that?" I asked, knowing what I'd heard from Capps and Bringloe in the back.

"I'm good," Capps said.

"Same here," Bringloe added. "Let's just get it done."

The LZ was still hot as we descended and set up for an approach. The bad guys shooting at our friendlies down below us were likely the same ones who had shot Wilson and Langa's Blackhawk full of holes. They weren't the kind of people to shoot and scoot. They had patience and discipline. They were perfectly willing to trade their lives for ours. They knew the value of shooting down an American aircraft, and the red crosses on our fuselage meant nothing to them beyond a good aiming point. In a weird way as the guy at the controls of their intended target, I harbored a soldierly respect for that.

The AQ and Taliban forces we fought in Afghanistan were different than the enemy I'd encountered in Iraq. In Iraq, the bad guys were a more conventional enemy. They relied on IEDs, spray and pray gunning, using familiar tactics against us. In The Stan, the fighters would do practically anything, taking all kinds of stupid risks, to engage us. One time my buddy and I had picked up a young gunshot victim. Somebody in her village had shot a little seven-year-old girl just to lure us into a pick-up so they could get a clear shot at an American helicopter. It was desperate fighting every time our guys on the ground were engaged in Afghanistan, and the only upside was that you knew where you stood with these guys. It was no-holds-barred all the time.

Through the NVGs, we could see small fights going on all over the hillside as we drilled down and kept an eye on the gunships racketing over the site. Those attack pilots had seen one medevac bird shot up today, and they were bound to do everything possible to see that the incident was not repeated. We were likely to take some fire on this mission, and I snuggled down a little lower in my armored seat. Up front, Kenny and I would at least be covered by some armor against small arms fire. In the back, it was a different deal for Capps and Bringloe. They had their flak vests and that was about it.

Julia Bringloe stared at the ground approaching on her side of the aircraft. It was going to be an interesting mission. She glanced across the cabin at Capps, who was focused on the web of tracers lancing through the dark on all sides of our flight path. She was going to get shot at on this one. It was inevitable, and it was not worth worrying about. She accepted the danger when she asked to become a flight medic. You had to accept that and just hope none of the incoming rounds hit home.

On this exhausting night over the Watapur Valley in Afghanistan, she was the only flight medic available. If that put her in the wrong place at the wrong time, there was not much to do about it. Her business was saving lives—going into the fight unarmed and focused on getting the wounded soldiers back to medical aid. That's what made all the difference to Julia Bringloe.

Julia adjusted her NVGs and watched the ground loom larger as Dustoff 7-3 turned for the approach to the wounded men waiting for her.

Up in the cockpit with my hands on the flight controls, I fought to concentrate. The battlefield below looked like what I'd imagined from Korea or Vietnam when I was playing soldier as a kid. It was tempting to just watch all the colorful

violence and imagine myself as a grunt in some historic battle. But this was Afghanistan, and all that colorful violence
was very real and very dangerous. I shook my head and
scanned the instruments while the rest of the crew looked for
something to tell us where the wounded were located.

It was chaos, and the chatter on the ground frequencies
didn't help us much. We were hearing shouts, screams, frantic orders and situation reports, all punctuated by the rattle
of gunfire in the background. I dropped us a little lower, staring through the NVGs at a grainy green world full of tree-
covered slopes, most of them too steep to climb. There were
wounded soldiers down there on one of them. But which
one? We passed over some fires that flared brightly in the
goggles and tracers flew all across a series of soft ruts,
ledges, and mud huts. Something caught my eye and I swore
I saw a cow burning down there. It was so unusual in my
experience that I let the aircraft drift closer to the blazing fire
on our left.

"Erik! Where you going, man?" Kenny brought me out
of it and I adjusted our flight path.

"Sorry. Coming right." We spotted the mud hut ahead of
us. That was our objective. "There they are. Everybody see
the *qalat*?" They'd all spotted it about the same time I did.

"You're clear right," Capps said as I pulled the cyclic
firmly to line us up on the mud hut. I gave the aircraft a little
left pedal and brought us onto a direct approach to the point
where we could see soldiers crouching around the structure.

"One minute," I called to Capps and Bringloe as Kenny
powered up the hoist and contacted the ground unit.

"Prodigal 1-7, this is Dustoff 7-3. We're one minute out
for your wounded," Kenny said.

"Roger, Dustoff. We have three soldiers for you. We'll
bring them up onto the roof." That might make things a little

easier on us during the hoist—a shorter ride for medic and patient. The ground guys were trying to give us a hand despite all their other problems in the fight. Never in my life did I imagine I'd be here, doing what I was about to do. I was a long way from the Blue Ridge Mountains of Virginia. I had to find some motivation for what I was about to attempt.

I reached down in my mind and found it. Mentally switching the memory of Tess back on, I imagined that she was this wounded soldier. I needed her here with me. I was committed to helping this perfect stranger, no matter what the consequences. Somewhere, somebody loved him as much as I love my wife. He and his friends were going home tonight—period.

We were trying to judge the best altitude for our hover when what seemed like eight or nine roman candles whizzed by right in front of my windshield from right to left. It jolted me, and it was all I could do not to wrestle the controls and hold us steady on the approach. One of the Kiowas working over the area was firing a steady stream of 2.75-inch rockets way too close, directly in my flight path. They were still working over the area as we tried to stay focused on the soldiers we could now see struggling with the wounded up on the flat roof of the mud hut they'd designated as our pick-up site.

"Steady, Erik…" Kenny watched the strobes on the Kiowas diving toward the ground ahead of us. "Just keep flying into it. They'll pull off before we get there."

It was hard to keep my eyes on the objective amid the shower of rocket trails that blazed like a curtain blocking our flight path. The Kiowas were pulling out of their runs now, but one final rocket flew past my nose and exploded on the ground below in a spectacular shower of sparks. The detonation cast an ugly orange glow throughout the cockpit.

Kenny pointed to the windscreen. "There's a stinking tree growing out of the roof of that hut, man! You see it?"

"I see it," I said. "That complicates matters a bit." I looked around the area for an alternative. We were approaching a large terraced hill about 150-feet wide at its base. The hills led up to the mud hut that looked like it was about to collapse. The offending tree was growing up from the interior and right through the roof. In back, Capps switched off the extra radios to eliminate the chatter in their headsets while he and Bringloe got ready for whatever we decided to do up in the cockpit. Kenny and I were trying to figure that out as we milled around over the pick-up location. So far, no one seemed to be shooting directly at us, but we weren't confident that that would hold. Ground units were still engaged on all sides of the fortified position down below on that hillside.

As we flew over the mud hut to get a closer look at our problem, I could see the structure was badly torn up by explosives and incoming fire. There was a cluster of soldiers using the walls as cover and a few others up on the roof with three wounded men. I came to a hover just far enough away from the tree to keep from hitting it, but our rotor wash was punishing for all concerned. The updraft was bouncing us around violently and the guys on the ground could barely stand. This was not the answer. A hoist was out of the question. If we fooled around with that, we'd likely lose the patients and medics and get ourselves shot down hovering at low level like a big, tempting bullseye. What we needed to do was get ourselves down onto that roof.

I called Bringloe and Capps off the hoist business and swung us around at low speed and altitude, trying to decide on the best approach. It looked like there just might be enough room on that roof to get one wheel down on it and still keep our tail rotor from smacking into the tree. If we could manage to set just one main landing gear down and hold it there, the grunts would be available to help us get the wounded aboard and we'd limit our exposure to enemy fire.

As we dove in to give it a try, I briefed the crew on our plan. There was nothing from the back except two terse Rogers. Capps and Bringloe knew what they'd have to do. Once we started slowly snuggling up to that roof with Kenny and I focusing on the big tree, they would have to guide us away from any other obstructions. And it looked like there were a bunch of those all around the area, including other tall trees and a string of threatening boulders just uphill from the structure where the wounded waited for us.

With Capps and Bringloe hanging out of the Blackhawk as far as their safety straps would allow on both sides of the cabin, I began a slow approach, aiming to just lightly tap one wheel on the roof. Our rotor wash was whipping hard on surrounding tall trees and the smaller ones were blown over almost parallel with the ground. We could see the soldiers clustered at the back of the roof. There was another group of them blasting away at something or someone in another stand of trees uphill from the hut where the structure nestled against the slope. Kenny kept an eye on that as I flew us closer, making subtle power adjustments. I needed to find a point of reference that would allow me to stay oriented while flying something this dicey, but I couldn't find anything. I was blind except for what I was hearing from the crew in back trying to guide us to a point where I could set one wheel on the roof.

"Keep it coming forward," Capps said. The wheel we wanted to plant on the roof was on his side of the aircraft, right behind me. "Come forward…three…two…one…hold hover! Down for four…three. You're drifting back! Stop! You're drifting right. Come left…two…one."

He was doing his best but conditions were all against us. The ground effect and our rotor wash were brutal, and at ultra-slow speed we were staggering around like a bunch of winos. "Kenny, I can't see a thing." We were still trying to steady up when we heard an urgent call from one of the Kiowas orbiting close overhead.

"I have the RPG team in sight," the Kiowa pilot called to someone on the ground who was directing him onto a target. "I'm engaging now." It was CPT Prichett, dropping down to save us. We saw his strobes blinking as he dove toward the ground on our left. There was a short burst of .50 caliber fire that ripped into an RPG gun team that had been aiming in on us from the rear. We heard the infantry confirm that the gunners were no longer a problem.

"Well, that's comforting." Kenny said. Capps and Bringloe in the back with their radios turned off had no idea how close we'd come to taking an RPG in our tail rotor from behind. I decided not to share the update and concentrate on getting the aircraft down on the roof. We heard a tense voice on the radio as we maneuvered back a bit to give it another try.

"Just get him off this mountain!" The soldier calling on the ground freq sounded desperate and we could hear the chatter of weapons firing on full-auto in the background. "Land, land, land!"

We were trying. "Clear left, right and above?" I maneuvered us toward the structure once again and called for guidance from Capps and Bringloe.

"Clear up left."

"Clear up right."

And the bouncing got worse.

"Let me try it, Erik," Kenny said reaching toward the controls.

"Yeah, you take it for a while. This place is just too much fun." I relinquished control and called the ground unit.

"Prodigal 1-7, this is Dustoff 7-3. It's tighter than we thought down there. Stand by..."

Kenny pulled us off to get a fresh start and the soldiers on the ground apparently misinterpreted our move.

"You're not coming back?" The voice on the radio was pleading rather than questioning.

"Of course we are," I told him. "We're not going to leave you guys down there. We're just gonna take another run at it from the north this time. Copy that?"

"Roger, Dustoff. Standing by." The relief in his voice was palpable. As Kenny maneuvered us for another shot at the one-wheel landing, I understood that we were all-in on this mission. None of us were leaving this mountain tonight without these patients. I ignored the part of me that was shouting to get out of that fight and silently recited the 23rd Psalm while Kenny lined us up for an approach from the opposite direction.

The northern route to the mud hut was even more confined than what we'd encountered on the other side. Kenny brought the nose up and staggered us slowly forward with trees brushing the belly of the Blackhawk. Bringloe could touch the treetops as she guided us in toward that roof. "Slide left...three...two... one...hold hover. You're gonna have to lift your tail in between two trees." Kenny established a solid, yet turbulent hover and pulled collective to lift the tail rotor. Out the window on my side, I could see streams of tracers that looked like they were close enough to touch and reflexively leaned in the other direction. Incoming or out-going, they were too close.

"Dustoff, Dustoff, be advised we are suppressing enemy close to your position at this time." The ground guys were trying to beat back the people shooting at us but things just seemed to get worse. At the ultra-slow speed we had to main-tain to finesse the approach, we were hovering ducks, and all the bad guys in the world wanted to take a crack at us. Two rockets slammed into the mountain just above us and their detonations sent a shockwave through the cockpit. These were bad guy rockets and not something the Kiowas fired. Kenny focused on the approach, fighting winds and blast ef-fect as the aircraft threatened to tumble down the mountain.

In the back, Bringloe ignored it all and tried to give him helpful direction. "Keep your tail up... stop! Come down...five... four...three...two. You have less than a foot on either side of your tail."

"Rrrrrroger," Kenny said. He was maintaining the "fa-çade of confidence" like a master. Any twitch right or left and we would lose the tail rotor to one of those trees and ride our bird into the ground. I'd never seen anything like this. I just kept my mouth shut and trusted that he hadn't reached the bottom of his bag of pilot tricks. If he bolo'ed this one, we were all dead.

We snaked in toward the roof, aiming the left main wheel at an edge of the roof. I didn't feel the touch, but Bringloe was staring at the closing distance between the wheel and the roof with a practiced eye. "Bring your left main over...two...one...left main is light." We were on the roof, balancing there on one wheel with the other wheel and most of the helicopter hanging over the edge without any kind of support except what we could coax out of the engines and rotors.

Just as Kenny established tenuous contact with the roof, two more rockets detonated close by, shaking the aircraft. Strobes were flashing out my right door, meaning the Kiowas were back in business. "It's just the Kiowas!" Kenny said. Two more rockets impacted on the hill above us and the Blackhawk shook violently. Much more of that and we might not be able to hold position. I thought about calling the Kiowas off, but that seemed like a bad idea since they were doing such a bang-up job of keeping the enemy from shooting us out of the air. Our tail rotor, and the entire back of our aircraft was now wedged in, just a couple feet away from two massive trees on either side. We had 10 or so rockets from the 58s impact in a 270-degree ring of fire, protecting us throughout the entire one-wheel landing. I decided to trust their vision and gunnery as Kenny Brodhead did a magical balancing act.

He had to keep the cyclic jammed to the left and while managing the collective to keep us heavy enough to hold position without dropping us onto the roof, which would collapse immediately beneath the weight of our Blackhawk. While he was doing that, he had to control our attitude in the horizontal plane. We would normally use the tail rotor pedals, but that might input too much torque, so Kenny managed it with the cyclic, trying to anticipate wind gusts before they happened. If he let the tail rotor smack into one of the trees less than a foot on either side of our tail boom, we'd spin out of control and likely kill everyone in the area as well as ourselves. While he fought for precise control, I watched that other tall tree jutting up from the roof. It was thick enough to spell disaster—and it was only about four feet outside our rotor disk.

If there was ever a dangerous position for a helicopter crew, this was it. We could only make the most delicate moves or changes in attitude while the massive battle raged around us. There were rockets impacting well within 100 meters of where we sat, and if they got any closer, we'd start catching shrapnel. As I grabbed for handholds on my door and above my head to keep from disturbing Kenny's efforts on the controls, I looked over at him and saw the brilliant rocket detonations flashing on his helmet. He was so tightly focused on what he was doing, he seemed to be in a trance.

If we didn't get on with it and get the wounded aboard, this stunt had a good chance of tanking. For some reason, the national anthem came to mind and I began to hum it to myself. It was stupid. It was also better than screaming. "Where are the casualties?"

"Coming now…" I craned over my seat to see Bringloe and Capps bunched by the door staring out into the dark.

"Get 'em on," Kenny said in a steady, firm voice. Capps and Bringloe needed no encouragement to hurry.

Bringloe grabbed the handle and slammed the cargo door open. She looked calm and moved with purpose. Waiting outside our aircraft were three ghostly figures back-lit by tracers and high explosive detonations. Two of those figures handed up a tall, skinny soldier covered in bloody bandages. His head was tilted back and I could see a thick battle dressing covering most of his face. This guy was wounded bad, but Julia would assess just how bad later. There were two more in similarly bad shape and Capps helped her get them all aboard. He jumped around getting them strapped into seats while Bringloe slammed the cargo door. She took a closer look at the bloodiest patient.

"Let's get out of here," she said. "This one is critical. He might not make it."

❧

That's what Kenny had been waiting for. He pulled the collective up carefully and we soared off the roof. He was pushing the engines now to gain speed and I monitored the systems. Whatever else happened, it wouldn't be as bad as the situation from which we'd just escaped. Kenny pulled us clear of the mountaintops and pointed the nose at the ground to gain airspeed. In moments we were cranking along at 160 knots on a fast dive toward the floor of the Pech River Valley and headed for our designated air station at A'bad.

"Prodigal 1-7, we have your wounded. Stay safe tonight."

As we steered toward help for the wounded in the back, we passed the flight of Kiowas that were still loitering over the area. "Nicely done, Dustoff," CPT Prichett said. His fellow Kiowa scout pilots had done a miraculous job of protecting us and they understood what we'd done and what we'd been through to get it done. I tried to smile but my jaw muscles wouldn't cooperate. They were worn out from all the teeth-clenching I'd done over the past hour.

In the back, Julia Bringloe was examining the patient in the worst shape under the beam of her flashlight. It was the skinny kid, and he was bad off, on that ragged edge where it could go either way. "I don't think this one's gonna make it," she said quietly.

That pushed us to try and fly faster. The guy in the back was going to need the best trauma care available, and that meant we'd head for the aid station at A'bad. We gave the Blackhawk a full head of steam, cautiously approaching engine limitations. I glanced down at the temperature gauges. The indicators were crawling past green and into the yellow caution zone. *Good enough*, I thought. We'd be on the ground before the engines overheated and the temperature control forced an engine flameout to prevent a fire. Still, if we had to trade an engine for a soldier's life, it was a no-brainer.

As we pushed on through the night, Julia Bringloe was doing everything she could to keep the casualty alive. Most of his lower face was missing on the right side. He'd been hit with a wicked burst of AK fire at very close range. She shouted for Capps to pass her the aid bag and then began to rummage around for what she needed. The man was leaking blood under the dressings applied by the ground medic and he was having trouble breathing. Bringloe drafted one of the less severely wounded soldiers and showed him how to keep pressure on an area to help staunch the bleeding. After poking through the bloody flesh and broken teeth, trying to get an emergency airway into the man, she decided his nose was the best option. If she had a little more time, if the soldier wasn't in such bad shape, she could have cut into his throat and made an airway below the mess on his face, but she had to settle for the nose tube and let the medics at the aid station do the cutting.

We radioed to let them know we had an urgent aboard and did our best to describe the man's wounds so they could be ready for him. Julia moved over to take a look at the other wounded soldiers. They were both shrapnel wounds and wouldn't need her help. She checked their bandages for leaks and then went back to monitor the critical man's vital signs.

The landing lights were a pale green and the A'bad landing pad looked like the deck of an aircraft carrier as we called for emergency clearance, kicked the tail out to the right, and skidded down onto the FST landing pad. In the dust storm kicked up by our rotor wash, five medics came scrambling toward us carrying stretchers. Bringloe hopped out to help get the casualties into the aid station while Capps got the aircraft ready for hot gas.

We'd need to get over to the FARP for fuel before we did any more flying, but I was in no hurry to move. I needed a breather away from the controls and so did Kenny. I could feel long, cold rivulets of sweat pouring out from under my helmet and down my back. I hadn't noticed that during the mission. Now I was oozing sweat. I was in a strange place between jubilation and exhaustion and my stomach churned. I wanted to get out of that rattletrap, upchuck and walk away, find a bed somewhere and collapse. Kenny felt the same way. A glance was all we needed to empathize. I just shrugged and massaged the sore muscles at the back of my neck. We were still the only medevac bird, and we would be doing some more flying shortly.

Julia Bringloe came limping out of the aid station on her bad leg and hopped into the cabin. "Doc says he's gonna make it," she said as she collapsed into her seat. "Another few minutes and we'd have lost him." That made it all worth whatever we did and would yet have to do this night. To give Kenny a little rest, I lifted us over to the FARP and we refueled. When we had enough to last for a while, I called us clear and headed back for FOB Joyce. On the way, I took a look at our EDM or Electronic Data Manager, a device we carried that showed us a moving map of the area and also let us send and receive text messages. We had a text from the command at J'bad. Terry O'Brien and his crew had made it up on an Assault Blackhawk just before the weather closed. We were due to swap out with them when we were mission complete at Joyce.

I shared the good news with the crew. There was no cheering. We were too tired to celebrate much beyond the simple joy of survival. As the lights of FOB Joyce came into view, I gave myself one last moment to think about Tess before I turned off the mental switch. *I will see you again, sweetheart.*

We handed the aircraft over to O'Brien's crew and staggered toward the tents for some sleep. As we collapsed, the battle was still raging up in the Watapur Valley. An infantry platoon was headed into the fight aboard a Chinook as reinforcements for the beleaguered troops on the ground. Things were about to go from bad to worse in Operation *Hammer Down.*

CHAPTER 9: REINFORCEMENTS

The thing is, helicopters are different from planes. An airplane by its nature wants to fly, and if not interfered with too strongly by unusual events or by a deliberately incompetent pilot, it will fly. A helicopter does not want to fly. It is maintained in the air by a variety of forces and controls working in opposition to each other, and if there is any disturbance in this delicate balance the helicopter stops flying immediately and disastrously. There is no such thing as a gliding helicopter. This is why being a helicopter pilot is so different from being an airplane pilot and why, in general, airplane pilots are open, clear eyed, buoyant extroverts, and helicopter pilots are brooders, introspective anticipators of trouble. They know that if something bad has not happened, it is about to.
—Harry Reasoner, 16 February, 1971
ABC Evening News

Watapur Valley
26 June 2011

A COLD WIND SWEPT down over the peaks above him as the young soldier from the 1ˢᵗ Platoon of Havoc Company squatted, surveying the long slope of forested hillside below their perch. It was supposed to be summer, but it was always chilly in the thin air at this altitude in the Afghanistan mountains. His unit had been hit hard up here trying to pry Taliban fighters out of several compounds. It had been a brutal, exhausting day of non-stop combat, but they had the wounded out and were anxiously expecting reinforcements. Once they got more grunts on the ground, they were slated to make a night attack downhill to rescue the Bravo Company platoon that was cut off and surrounded by the enemy.

Somewhere up in the black sky, there was supposed to be helicopters carrying fresh men, but the young soldier couldn't see much except for a few low, drifting clouds reflecting snatches of pale moonlight. And then he heard the distinctive whop and rattle of twin-bladed helicopters echoing off the peaks. A grizzled, veteran sergeant standing nearby keyed his handset.

"Bison 4-2, Chaos 7. Understand you are inbound from the north. Buzz-saw on the LZ."

"Is that them, Top?" The young soldier stood and checked the infrared chem-light on a length of parachute cord. It was called a buzz-saw in Army jargon. He was due to swing it around his head as a marker for the helicopters carrying reinforcements.

"Yep; they're coming." The First Sergeant pointed at the clearing below them. "Crack that chem-light and get ready to bring 'em in…"

As the sergeant watched the young soldier scramble down the hillside toward the clearing, he mentally counted the troops he had left. There weren't that many—a lot fewer than he had when Operation *Hammer Down* started. They'd been through a lot and it wasn't over until they managed to rescue or relieve the company's stranded platoon. He had buddies in that unit and he felt for them, stuck in a fire-trap after being ambushed as they moved down the mountain toward the valley floor. The problem was the terrain. They were trying to clear some Taliban training camps, and they ran into a rabbit warren of caves and heavily fortified positions all over the mountainside. And those positions were prepared by veteran fighters to funnel attackers into killing zones.

It had been a meat-grinder of a fight all day as they tried to push downhill. Eventually, it developed into a street brawl with his troops so close to the enemy that they could hear the Taliban changing magazines. If anyone needed a textbook example of what the Army called Close Quarters Battle, this was it. Two of their guys had to play dead to save themselves when the Taliban counterattacked during the day. They'd lost about half of them in the fight, and they desperately needed replacements before they tried to push on farther downhill. He was running through squad assignments in his mind when the first Chinook popped up over the mountaintops behind him.

To the north of the soldiers on the ground, chugging along at 12,000 feet, an Army National Guard CH-47D Chinook swooped over the peaks. The crew of Bison 4-2 was flying one of the Army's best—and oldest—heavy-lift aircraft capable of operating at extreme altitudes. The venerable Chinook was once an endangered species, ready to be retired—but it was proving its worth in the mountains of Afghanistan and now had a long career ahead of it again.

The pilot spotted the whirling IR signal through his NVGs in a clearing below and called the other Chinook on the mission to let them know he had the LZ in sight. "Bison 4-3, 4-2 has the buzz-saw. We're gonna set her down on the north side of the LZ and then make an early left crosswind departure toward the Kunar to link up. How copy?"

"Bison 4-3 copies all. Advise when you're clear."

The lead Chinook crew ran through the landing check-list and called their guys in the back with an estimated time to arrival on the LZ. "We're good back here, sir," the crew chief responded, and then shoved his way through the 57 tightly packed grunts to let them know they would be of-floading in a couple of minutes. The LZ was cold—at least so far. The crew chief checked his gunners, one at the door opposite his, manning a duplicate of the M-240 machinegun that he used when he wasn't otherwise occupied. The Stinger or tail-gunner was in position, feet outstretched in front of him as he nestled behind his worn M-240H that suppressed enemy shooters during the vulnerable time when they were pulling out of a landing zone.

As they descended for their final approach, the pilots and crew could see tracer rounds zipping across firefights down in the valley. It was distant and unrelated to their mission of getting the grunts in back on the ground, so they drove on, leaving that up to the infantry and the Apache gunships that were flying escort at altitude above the LZ. Below Bison 4-2, treetops began to wave in their rotor wash. They were heavy and their twin rotors were chewing hard on the thin air at 10,000 feet, trying to support the load. The command pilot dialed in a little more thrust control to increase pitch on the blades and give them a better bite while guiding the air-craft down toward the infrared marker with subtle input on his tail-rotor pedals. He was short final now, glancing be-tween his instrument displays and swiveling his head to in-crease the limited peripheral scan of only 40 degrees available when he wore his NVGs. It was like looking through a toilet-paper roll, but he was used to it and knew the tricks involved with night flying. He took another look at the buzz-saw, estimated the range, and called his crew chief.

"Two minutes, guys!"

In the back of the Chinook, the crew chief and door-gunners held up two fingers and shouted over the roar of the engines and the clatter of the rotors. There was nothing to indicate this would be anything more than your textbook night insertion. Bison 4-2 dropped through the night sky into turbulent air. The heavy helicopter was just starting translation from forward flight to a hover when the routine shattered.

There was a burst of punishing downdraft that broke over the peaks just as Bison 4-2 was trying to establish a hover and settle into the landing zone. It was not something the crew in the cockpit could see or anticipate. While they were just adjusting into ground effect for a landing, the gust of deadly wind hit them from above and pushed on the aircraft like a plunger. In back, the crew chief tumbled and sprawled across the legs of their grunt passengers. Bison 4-2 was being shoved toward the ground despite what the flight controls demanded.

"This ain't good!" The command pilot stated the obvious. "We're settling!"

"Go around, go around!" the crew chief shouted into the ICS and tried to reach his station at the door. He had enough hours to know this was not a workable approach.

In the cockpit, there were master caution lights flashing red on the dash panel and the pilot told his co-pilot to get on the controls with him in an attempt to muscle the Chinook back into control. "We're in a downdraft—I need some help here!" They both fought to restore lift as the rogue wind drove them toward the ground out of control.

They heard the sound of the low rotor warning horn blaring in their ears.

And that was all for Bison 4-2. The aircraft lost lift and the aft rotor shredded at impact with the trees surrounding the LZ. The big blades shattered, sending the Chinook into a fatal spin and blowing splinters all across the area. The two rotor systems devoured each other as the aircraft bent and ripped apart.

Inside the Chinook, crew and passengers were tossed around like dice rattling in a cup. As the fuselage of the aircraft twisted, torque sent shockwaves through the passenger cabin. Grunts and crewmen bashed into each other in a bloody sprawl. Many of them were too hurt to do anything but bleed or groan. Those that were able set to work trying to get themselves and everyone else out of the wreckage.

Across the LZ, the acrid smell of JP-8 jet fuel began to waft in a cloud. Before many of the grunts on the ground could reach the crash, that volatile fuel burst into flames. Sparks from the Chinook's electrical systems lanced into pools of gas spewing from ruptured lines and a small fire lit up the night over the LZ. Grunts from all sides of the LZ perimeter rushed toward the wreck hoping to rescue any survivors.

Shaking his head in disbelief in the tree line next to the chaos, the First Sergeant wondered what else could go wrong and keyed his radio. "All stations this net, be advised we have an aircraft down on LZ Dragonfly. We are attempting to extract survivors." He took a deep breath and repeated the bad news for everyone in the Watapur Valley. "I say again— the Chinook with our other Chaos element has crashed on the LZ. Break. We'll need Dustoff. Expect nine-line requests to follow."

An officer watching from a nearby position keyed his radio. "Copy all, Chaos 7. We'll be alerting Dustoff immediately."

CHAPTER 10: HIGHER GROUND

**If you want to grow old as a pilot, you have to know
when to push it and when to back off.**

—Chuck Yeager

26 June 2011

HOURS BEFORE THE disastrous Chinook crash up in the Watapur, we were in the process of handing off the support mission to our relief crew and trying to sort out our schedules and logistics. Chief Warrant Officer 3 Terry O'Brien and his crew made it up to give us some relief, but they didn't bring a spare Blackhawk. We'd have to share 9-4-4, the old reliable airframe that had been flying all day and most of the night as Dustoff 7-3.

At the time we made the aircrew switch, there was only one medevac mission on the board. Terry O'Brien, along with his co-pilot Chief Warrant Officer 2 Dan Jarc, Crewchief Specialist Todd Demery, and First Sergeant Brian Peplinski, our company's senior flight medic, got airborne to handle that. I was tired and needed some sleep, I was now the MEDEVAC Air Mission Commander for Operation *Hammer Down*. I had to figure a few things out before I could join the rest of my crew in the sleeping tent.

Sergeant Johnny Reyes was keeping our maps and status boards updated as usual. He gave me a rundown on what was happening up in the mountains with Operation *Hammer Down,* where units seemed to be in a brief hiatus. Reyes indicated there was a plan to lift more grunts into the Watapur aboard a flight of Chinooks escorted by Apaches, and things would probably heat back up when those reinforcements arrived. Maybe it would be a slow night and we could manage the specified hours of rest before we had to relieve O'Brien's crew and get airborne again.

I stood by the maps and watched as Reyes was relieved by Specialist Fittos on the mission computers. It had been a stressful time for Reyes who served as our sole source of information through a grueling day and night. While we flew, he handled practically everything else for our detachment. He told me every time he tried to get away for a little break, the phone would ring or some problem would arise that he needed to handle. Staff infantry officers would call our CP wondering why we weren't flying through the clouds to get the wounded. Reyes had to explain that Blackhawks didn't have radar, and that we can't see through clouds. It was a typical duty day for SGT Reyes and he laughed a lot more than he complained as we walked toward the sleeping tent.

When we got there, my crew was already asleep. I tried to make as little noise as possible, but I think a grenade could have detonated and they would not have noticed. I had grown fond of Blackhawk 9-4-4 and hoped O'Brien didn't break or bend it while I slept. If that happened, we'd be in real trouble.

A few hours later, I woke with a start. I'd had some sort of premonition, or maybe it was just a nightmare. By the time I rolled over trying to resettle, bad news broke the silence in the sleeping tent. Fittos called from ops. "Mr. Sabiston to the CP." Herding our weary crew along toward the flight line, I checked my watch. It was still dark in the early morning hours, and we weren't legal to fly yet according to regulations. I wondered why we got the call. What was up with O'Brien and his guys?

Fittos let me know as we stumbled into the ops area. "Sorry, sir—but Mister O'Brien and his crew have run out of duty day." Apparently, they'd had a busy time while we were trying to log our required hours of rest. So we had one crew that had to rest, one crew that hadn't had enough rest, and one aircraft that had barely shut-down for the past 24 hours. Wonderful.

Looking around at my crew, I could see they knew the score and were ready to jump into the inbound bird as soon as I gave the word. "What's the deal?" I slumped down on a couch and waited for Fittos to fill in the details.

"One of the Chinooks crashed up on a high LZ during that insert mission,' he said. "Mr. O'Brien and his guys have been hauling injured grunts and aircrew for hours."

"How bad was it?"

"Pretty bad—no fatalities but there were a lot of guys banged up—and the Chinook is trashed. It's a total loss."

Kenny Brodhead was checking the weather as I got up to look at the maps. Not much had changed in the tactical picture. The friendly units were pretty much where they had been the last time I looked. The crash and subsequent rescue efforts seemed to have put the offensive on hold for a while, but I knew that wouldn't last. And there were still some medevacs waiting for lift out of that mountainside LZ.

"Weather's crappy to the south," Kenny told me, "but it looks OK here."

"How many patients?" I looked over at SGT Julia Bringloe who was scanning the nine-line that was coming in from the grunts on the ground.

"Eight hoists waiting, and three need to go now."

"OK, let's get geared up to go as soon as it lands. We'll launch once they fuel and bring 9-4-4 back here. Most of the medevacs will go to A'bad, so give them a call and let them know we'll be bringing in some more soon. They'll need to clear the emergency room."

While the crew scrambled, I picked up the phone and called CPT Wilson to update him on the situation and discuss our options. We badly needed another aircraft and another relief crew wouldn't hurt either.

"Weather's nasty between us and Bagram," Wilson told me when I ran through our problems. "Pilot reports are saying less than three-hundred-feet ceilings and it's probably gonna get worse. I'm trying to get another crew up there to help, but it all depends on the weather."

"How about 7-2? We really need another bird up here in case something breaks on the one we're flying."

"She's seen better days. Maintenance is working on it now, but I don't think it will be ready to fly in time to give you a hand."

"You know this is making it tough in the duty day situation…" I said,

He continued, "I know. You're gonna have to cut some corners and do the best you can to support the mission. Just take it slow and be safe."

"Hey, sir—it's me!" I could hear the tension in CPT Wilson's voice and I wanted to reassure him we had the situation under control. When we hung up, I looked over at Capps and Bringloe. "We're gonna have to hold the line until they get some breathing room. CPT Wilson is doing everything he can to get us another aircraft and crew." They both just nodded and went back to work preparing to fly when O'Brien landed.

The sun was starting to peek over the mountaintops when
O'Brien arrived at the LZ. At least we'd be able to fly this
mission without NVGs. That was something. The crew
crawling out of the aircraft looked exhausted. O'Brien
hauled his tall frame out of the right seat and looked around
at his crew gathering their weapons and equipment. He was
a big bear of a man with broad shoulders and a six-foot-five
frame. His size made the Blackhawk look small, like one of
those little coin-operated kid rides you see in front of a K-
Mart. I walked out to get an update before I replaced him in
the aircraft.

"Dude, that Chinook is trashed!" Terry said and filled me
in on what we'd encounter when we got up to the Watapur.
When he finished, I walked over and said hello to Terry's
co-pilot. I liked Jarc. He was among the youngest officers in
our outfit, and he'd been picked on mercilessly by the older
pilots during the early stages of our deployment. He took it
all with aplomb and generally gave as much harassment as
he got. I remembered once when Aaron Michaud had given
him a hard time and Dan fought back by salting Michaud's
library of technical manuals with hundreds of pictures of
Jodie Foster, one of Aaron's least favorite celebrities. I'd
gleefully given him a hand with some of those payback
pranks.

While we talked, Capps arrived to confer with fellow
crew chief Todd Demery, one of the best in our unit. His wife
was an active duty soldier also stationed in Afghanistan. As
far as I knew, they hadn't managed to see each other yet. Dan
Jarc told me Demery had a tough night. On one of their hoist
efforts, the safety strap that tied his medic to the JP broke
loose and he fell off the hook. Demery watched in horror as
the monkey strap on his medic's gear was all that saved him

from a long, fatal fall. He walked by me with his helmet and grinned. "Busy night, preacher…"

Kenny Brodhead arrived at the aircraft with an intelligence update he'd gotten from SGT Reyes and it didn't sound good. It was no wonder the fight was so hot and heavy on Operation *Hammer Down*. The estimates of the number of AQ and Taliban fighters in the area near the Pakistan border were short of the reality on the ground. The troops maneuvering up in those mountains were finding themselves outnumbered at every turn. Hence the call for reinforcements, and there would be more on the way as the day progressed. They were encountering shooters from several different nations, all devoted to holding ground and killing Americans. During the periods when allied forces were involved elsewhere, the bad guys had opened a pipeline from bases in Pakistan, and now they were pouring over the border in a flood. Even worse, the main LZ was in the middle of the main enemy supply route. Field commanders were rethinking the whole mission and rushing more troops into the fight.

As we climbed into the cockpit to begin the start-up procedures, I took a look at the sky. The weather in the northwest looked bad with thick, soupy clouds rolling down the mountainsides. We had to fly in that direction. When we got power to the Blackhawk, I tuned the radios to see what I could hear from helicopters in the air. We caught a weather report from a Kiowa pilot over the Watapur as our blades began to turn and Bringloe and Capps mounted the aircraft for departure.

"This is Joker 5-8. The valley is socked in pretty good. We just did a hand-off and the pilots are calling ceilings broken at four-hundred feet with tops well above ten thousand. It's a mess out here—completely impassable."

Even if we managed to find our objective in the valley, we wouldn't be able to see anything on the ground. Kenny glanced over at me. "Might as well shut her down," he said. "We aren't going anywhere until the weather clears up in the valley."

We shut down the engines and stowed our flight gear in the seats. "I'm gonna call weather and try to get a forecast," I told Kenny. "You guys hold on here and let's see how long it's gonna be."

Back in the ops area, I grabbed a phone and got through to the Air Force weather-guessers. A bubbly sounding female answered my questions after I listened to a few minutes of poetic description concerning storm cells and high pressure troughs. The weather was due to clear in a few hours. I hung up and walked back to the aircraft where my crew was waiting to see if we would fly.

"Everybody unload and take a break. We'll call you when the weather starts to cooperate." It didn't take them long to head back to the sleeping tent. If there was anything good about the weather front from our perspective, it meant we might get some more sleep and catch up for a regulation duty day.

I checked my watch again and thought about the regulations that dictated how long Army flight crews could fly without adequate rest. It was a matter of some concern, and the regs were enforced as much as possible for good reasons. In the Army helicopter community, we all knew the stories about crews in Vietnam that had flown themselves to death—literally—operating at high tempos on short rest. You can't just pull a helicopter over to the side of the road and catch a cat-nap. A helicopter can be very unforgiving of mistakes made by exhausted pilots.

However, any delay meant that wounded or injured guys on the ground would have to wait—and there was the possibility that some of them wouldn't survive. That was unacceptable to any Dustoff crew. The cargo we flew on medevac missions was America's most precious asset: the nation's soldiers, the sons and daughters who depended on us for rescue and prompt medical attention. That's a sacred trust among Dustoff crews. We weren't just Army Aviators, we were soldiers just like the people doing the fighting up in that valley. When we flew a mission and a fellow soldier died before we arrived, or on the aircraft during the evacuation flight, it was as if a part of us died also. No one was going to fault us for taking advantage of the weather hold to catch up on crew rest, but that didn't make it any easier to sleep. I prayed hard for good weather.

While the rest of Dustoff 7-3 caught up on some shuteye, I paced the ops area and did busy work. I constantly checked for weather updates, but nothing much changed for three long hours. I kept thinking about the grunts waiting for us on the ground. They couldn't take a break no matter what the weather was over the battlefield. As I was reaching for the phone to make yet another call to the weather forecasters, I heard rotors outside and walked over to see a couple of Kiowas pushing into the Kunar Valley in the direction of the Watapur. By the time I got back to his desk, Johnny Reyes already had the phone in hand and a connection made to the main weather office at Jalalabad.

The same female NCO was on the line sounding flustered by all the update calls she was getting from pilots all over the area. I asked her for a brief on the Watapur Valley. She tersely informed me the ceiling was slightly better at 7,500 hundred feet but the mountaintops were still socked in by dense clouds. We could get up into the valley but not up onto the high ground where our patients waited. On the other hand, it seemed to be clearing and those Kiowas were willing to risk it.

"We're outta here!" I grabbed the mission sheet and pointed at Reyes. "Call 'em, Johnny!" I was out the door and running for the flight line. Before I got to the helicopter, I caught sight of Kenny, Bringloe, and Caps pounding along to join me.

"Clear the P!" I yelled. As I put on my helmet and gloves, Kenny indicated that he had the controls. We felt the oscillation as the rotors melded into a transparent disk. Bringloe and Capps hopped in and called that they were in and secure. As Kenny got us airborne, I called ops to let them know we were back on mission.

"Ops, Dustoff 7-3 is departing now for the three casualties previously briefed."

"Roger—and be advised that we got an update. Another one just dropped and they're saying the patient looks pretty bad. It's urgent. How copy?"

"Got it. Send us the grid. We'll get him first, then the other three and anybody else that needs to get out of there."

When I punched in the grid for the urgent evac, the GPS bearing pointer instantly swung to the top of my compass card. The wounded man was high up in the steep brown cliffs covered with clouds. It looked like someone had thrown a big comforter over the mountains in the Watapur Valley. As we flew around the soup, the radios were squawking with transmissions from ground units trying to maneuver and find each other in the same mess. Our contact down there was another Prodigal unit, and I dialed up their frequency to give them a call.

"Prodigal 3-6, Dustoff 7-3. We're five minutes out for patient pickup. Visibility is poor. Better use smoke to mark the LZ."

"Negative, Dustoff. We have enemy nearby so smoke is not an option. Look for a VS-17 panel."

"Well, that's gonna be interesting," I said as we followed the position indicator and began to search through the mist for a marker panel.

"It's on your side," said Kenny. "You have the controls."

"I have the controls," I said.

Capps finally spotted it in an area that was littered with massive boulders piled up at various heights like tinker toys. Surrounding that rocky field was yet another stand of tall pines. Our patient was somewhere in those trees, and we'd have to keep the aircraft at a respectful altitude for the hoist operation. Capps would have to lower Bringloe into the rocky area and then we would need to reposition the Black-hawk to retrieve her and the urgent medevac. It was beginning to look like a repeat of the earlier hoist that smashed her leg.

She got on the ground safely riding the JP and then rushed into the trees to check on the patient. We waited to see where she wanted us for the pick-up. She emerged from the treeline with a couple of soldiers carrying the wounded man. She pointed to a semi-clear spot, retrieved the JP and hoist cable, and began to strap the patient in for the lift. She glanced around trying to decide how best to make the hoist amid the big rocks and looming tree limbs. When she strad-dled the JP with her arms wrapped around the patient, Julia gave Capps a signal and he began to retrieve our load.

Bringloe had her legs stuck straight out, hoping to use them as shock absorbers if they started to oscillate and got too close to a limb or one of those big boulders. Naturally, that's exactly what happened and she did a terrific job in a sort of reverse-rappel when the JP got too close to a big rock face. Capps muscled the cable into submission as Julia and her patient cleared the rocks and then we heard a welcome call.

"Medic is at the cabin. Medic and patient are in. You're clear!"

I glanced through the overhead windows above the cockpit that we called the greenhouse to spot any obstacles in the way of our main rotor and then slowly added power to lift us clear. We had our urgent patient safely aboard, heading for A'bad and the medical care he needed.

We got our urgent patient to the aid station in record time and waited while Bringloe got him situated and briefed the doctors. She was back in five minutes with a report that the man was going to survive his wounds. We lifted into a pedal-turn and headed back toward the valley where we had three more patients still on the ground. The weather was still junk up in the Watapur, so we got hold of the infantry unit holding the wounded soldiers and asked for smoke to mark the LZ. They told us we'd have to do another search for an air panel. They were fresh out of smoke grenades. The best they could do was a VS-17 panel.

"Here we go again," I said to Kenny as I stared down through the ground fog that was still rolling down the mountainside.

"They've been marking LZs for speedballs and marking targets for the gunships since this op started," he said. "No wonder they don't have any smoke left." A speedball was a prepared load of ammo, rations, water, medical supplies, and other consumables that was rigged onto a padded pallet that could be pushed out of a helicopter without the danger of having to land in close proximity to enemy forces. There had been a lot of speedballs delivered on Operation *Hammer Down* before the weather closed in and grounded most of the re-supply efforts. We were often asked to help carry ammo or replacement weapons, although that was prohibited under regulations. We were unarmed and involved in missions of mercy—not that it meant much to the Taliban and AQ guys who loved to shoot at medevac helicopters moving slow or holding a hover. We were excellent targets. We carried M-4 carbines for personal protection in case of a shoot-down, but we did not carry defensive weapons like door gunners which might be handy in suppressing the LZs we approached under fire. There was some griping about that in the Big Army, but I preferred to avoid the extra weight. It kept us light and maneuverable at the high altitudes we worked in Afghanistan.

This was going to involve a hoist at an extremely high mountain peak, so I needed to do some math and see about our power-to-weight ratios. I ducked my head to crunch some data and turned the controls over to Kenny.

"You've got it, brother. Right front is inside to check the numbers."

"Left front is increasing scan," Kenny said taking the controls and watching out my side of the aircraft as well as his while I was otherwise employed. It looked like we could do it safely, but we would have to stay high. I powered up the hoist, let Capps know the deal, and popped my head back outside, scanning the ever rising terrain.

"We're five minutes out."

Capps and Bringloe did their buddy checks and she mounted the JP to prepare for the descent when we went into a hover over the pick-up spot.

Kenny spotted the VS-17 panel moments later and pointed at a spot where fog was swirling in our rotor wash. "There it is—off to the left front about eleven-thirty."

"It's gonna be tight," I said. "I'll call your torque." We had very little power to play with at this altitude and even moderate demands made by the flight controls might be more than the Blackhawk's engines could deliver. If we got ourselves into an over-torque situation the rotors would droop—or slow down—significantly. When helicopter rotors do that, the aircraft they are supporting drops like a rock. Blackhawks make lousy gliders.

As we chugged into an approach, I ran the numbers again in my head trying to add what I thought might be the weight of the three men we were going to carry. Math was never my strong suit, and I'd managed to fail pre-algebra twice in college. At this point, my computations meant more than a lousy grade in a classroom. If I got the numbers wrong we might die. I was full of second thoughts and doubts, but I had to go with what I believed was correct. *This is what I get for being a punk in high school and not paying attention*, I thought, as Kenny interrupted.

"We'll have a tailwind from this angle because of the obstacles, but it should be OK."

It sounded crazy to me, but it turned out to be a smart approach. The wind was shooting up the mountainside from the valley below and that would give us some extra lift. The way Kenny was approaching the LZ, our natural departure direction with the extra weight of the patients would be to the right. Falling away in that direction would add speed to the rotors and that would provide a fraction of extra power. I felt a lot better with Kenny Brodhead sitting across the cockpit from me.

We pulled into a hover trying to hold a shuddering aircraft at 60 feet over the ground below. The radio squawked to let us know the soldiers on the ground had us in sight. Capps boomed the hoist out and Julia Bringloe began her ride down to gather up the first of our three patients. In a short time, while we kept our eyes on the engine monitoring instruments, Capps let us know our flight medic was on the ground. He was getting good at this stuff and put Julia down right between a spread of tall boulders, despite the wind gusts that were hammering at our fuselage.

In the cloud of blowing sand and dust below us, Julia finally found the three wounded soldiers kneeling in a trench line. None of them were hit very bad, but their wounds needed attention to avoid infection or other complications. She quickly got the first man hooked up and then dropped back down on the JP to get the next man. The process kept us in that shaky, wind-buffeted hover for a long time, and I was worried about being a static target. We could see soldiers in a perimeter watching in all directions to provide cover for us, but it only took one True Believer with an RPG to cause a disaster. We'd been holding at 60 feet for five minutes or so when Bringloe made her final trip. The soldiers asked her to take some extra gear they had laying around, but Julia said no, knowing that it would weigh us down, droop the rotor, and kill us all. They pushed her further, but after some choice words, they backed off. SGT Bringloe was in no mood for good-idea fairies. I'd had soldiers ask us to pick up a 10,000-pound vehicle with our 600-pound-rated hoist, but that only works in the movies. She had decided to bring up the biggest wounded man last and a smaller portion of the soldiers' gear, so their buddies wouldn't have to hump it up and down the hills. Up front, we just fought the wind and watched distant firefights going on at other locations on the hillside above and below us.

"Medic's on the JP now; cabling up with the last one." Capps sounded worried so I asked him how it was going.

"They're really heavy," he said. "She's got their rucks and gear."

Bringloe had her legs wrapped around the patient and two heavy rucksacks suspended from her arms. It was too much for the hoist which had reached its mechanical limits. The high-speed winching gear disengaged and the lift turned into a crawl as the hoist motor automatically dropped into a slow low gear to handle the weight.

"They're still coming up," Capps reported. "But it's really slow."

"I can tell," Kenny said over ICS. We could feel the strain on the struggling hoist.

"We're going to droop the rotor!" I shouted needlessly. The mountains suddenly rose taller in my windshield. On the instrument panel we could see the rotor RPM dip slightly. I felt the aircraft begin to sink as Kenny took action. He stomped the right pedal and brought the back side of our rotor disk into the updrafts. The Blackhawk bucked forward and then the nose rose slightly. The aircraft held its position. We were stable and the rotor was in the green.

"A thing like that will wake you right up, won't it?" Kenny was grinning again under his mustache.

"She's coming in now," Capps said. "Medic and patient are at the door. Medic and patient are in the cabin. That's it."

"I'm going to try and snoop through this little cut in the peak," Kenny said nodding toward a notch in the mountaintop on our left. It didn't look big enough for us to slide through without smacking the blades on the rocks, and it didn't seem like a solid plan with only about 5 percent power left until we hit max torque available and drooped the rotors. On the other hand, this was Kenny, so I kept my mouth shut and watched as he lifted us toward his planned bolt-hole.

We drifted slowly upward, pushed mostly by air currents until we were level with and facing the notch. It felt like that gut-wrenching pause at the top of a rollercoaster ride just before the big plunge. Kenny nudged the controls and we slid through with just a few feet on either side of our main rotor disk. On the other side of the cut was a sheer 8,000-foot drop. My hate for heights swept over me and I wished I was flying instead of Kenny, but he was doing better than I could have done. As he nosed us over the drop, I grabbed the door and overhead grips to keep him from seeing how much my hands were shaking.

He pushed on the cyclic and we plummeted down the mountainside at about 30 degrees, which just happens to be the Blackhawk's absolute engineering limit. Rocks and trees on the mountainside blurred into an indecipherable mass as we dropped. As our airspeed increased, the rotor blades began to snap and pop in cleaner air. It sounded like a runaway machinegun. Kenny just kept grinning as he finally leveled us out above the floor of the valley and turned for a quick trip to the FST.

In an effort to let my stomach settle, I fiddled with the radios and then looked over at my co-pilot. "I don't know if I ever told you this, Kenny—but I hate heights."

At the landing pad outside the aid station, I watched SGT Julia Bringloe assist the medics in getting our patients inside for treatment. She looked ragged and her limp had gotten worse. Ten minutes later she looked a bit better, or at least a bit cleaner, when she came walking back to the Blackhawk. She was apologizing for the delay and said a female officer in the aid station told her to get cleaned up before she went back to duty. When she tried to refuse, the request became an order, so she washed a bit of the grime and gunk off her face and hands at one of the scrub sinks.

When she was settled in back alongside Capps, we lifted over to the FARP to take on some fuel. We still had non-critical patients waiting on the ground. I planned to pick them up and then try to recover the dead American platoon leader and Afghan interpreter. The LZ had to be cold before we could get to them. We were just about to get started on that when reliable old Blackhawk 9-4-4 finally had enough.

There was an ugly yellow light on the center advisory panel that said MASTER CAUTION and it was brightly lit. It was not something like that little Check Engine light that we all ignore in our cars. This was trouble. I scanned the panel again and read INP MDL LEFT HAND. What that told us was that a piece of the gears that transferred power from the left engine to the main transmission had broken off and bumped one of the sensor screens. It was a big enough chunk to cause the master caution warning, and we were not going to fly until it was checked and cleared or repaired.

"You got to be kidding me!" I screamed at the panel. "We don't need this now!"

"What are you waiting for?" Kenny looked over at me and shrugged. "Shut her down." He knew it was necessary, and so did I. If the transmission module was eating itself alive, we could do some serious damage by trying to fly. I shut down the left engine as we ground taxied off the fuel pad and into a clear spot where we finished shutting down the other engine. We were now completely out of flyable air-craft to support the medevac mission. I had been a crewchief once too—but I had to have a second opinion.

Leaving the crew with the damaged bird, I ran for the aid station and grabbed the first phone I saw. I got through to Alex, who was waiting for his broken bird to be fixed back at J'bad. When he got on the line, I told him what the situation was and he agreed we shouldn't try to fly.

"She's definitely grounded," he told me. "The good news is that the weather is clearing down here. We'll get up there as soon as we can and either clear 9-4-4 for flight or get you another bird. Tell Capps to pull the chip detector so I can inspect it."

I went back to the aircraft and passed the word. We wouldn't be going anywhere for a while, and there was time to get something to eat. While Capps worked on getting the aircraft ready for the maintenance check, Kenny sat on the cabin floor and watched him work. I could see his disappointment. Anybody who got hit and needed evacuation was out of luck until we got cleared or crewed up on a replacement aircraft.

While Bringloe went to the break room in search of something to eat, I distracted myself with chores. There was a line of soldiers sitting in chairs along one wall who needed to be taken out of the aid station to make room for other patients. They had been treated and cleared for transportation, so I worked on getting them rides back to their main base. Capps walked in about a half hour later and followed me back to the break room where Julia was packing up some food for all of us. It was standard fare: Cold sandwiches in Styrofoam containers and lukewarm sodas.

One of the surgeons, who had been treating wounded most of the night, was half asleep in a rump-sprung easy chair staring vacantly at something on the TV.

"How did that one with the face wounds make out?" That poor guy was the worst wounded we'd handled to date.

"Which one?" Apparently he'd seen more than one soldier with a damaged face on his shift.

"The one that was missing part of his jaw."

"Oh, him. Yeah, he's gonna be fine. He's probably on his way back to Germany by now. They've already started reconstructive surgery. Lost a ton of blood. Your medic saved his life for sure."

Julia didn't look up at the compliment. She quietly picked up the load of lunch boxes and headed for the door.

We brought food back to the bird, but nobody was anxious to get at it. Kenny, who was rumored to eat only Cinnamon Toast Crunch on deployment, just sipped a Diet Coke. I ate because I was hungry and needed energy, but I felt guilty about it. The guys waiting up there for us were eating less than what we had—if they were eating at all. When I finished, I crashed out on the cabin floor next to Kenny who was staring through the open cabin door in the direction of the Watapur Valley. Like all aviators, we were used to encountering mechanical problems, but this one hit me in the gut. Capps crawled under the Blackhawk to get out of the punishing sun and Bringloe trudged back to the aid station to see if she could lend the nurses and doctors a hand.

After a couple of hours, Alex Langa arrived from Jalalabad in another Blackhawk. The weather had cleared sufficiently for him to make the trip and he sped up to A'bad to see what we were facing with the only medevac bird available to support operations. He immediately got with Capps and took a look at the chip detector. He eyed a few metal slivers critically and decided we were good to go. Capps rapidly replaced the chip detector and buttoned us up for flight. We sent word for Julia as I spent a little time talking to Alex about our situation. It was late in the day and we would have to swap out with O'Brien's crew before much longer. What we needed was another Blackhawk sent up to FOB Joyce.

Alex didn't think that was going to happen. His aircraft was still in maintenance, he had to get the one he'd flown up back to J'bad where things had been heating up for units operating in that area. Things were tough all over Afghanistan. Langa was stuck with a growing list of maintenance chores himself and really needed to get rolling back toward our unit base. He made a detour on that trip to help us fly some of the soldiers from the aid station that were returning to duty and then took off heading south. We landed back at FOB Joyce near dusk and shut 9-4-4 down for the crew swap.

"She's all yours," I said to Dan Jarc as he and O'Brien relieved Kenny and me in the cockpit. "Keys are in the ignition."

They saddled up, cranked the engines, and disappeared into the gathering dark headed for the Watapur Valley. It had been another dangerous and frustrating day of flying for us, full of cheap thrills and ulcer-generating problems, but that's what you sign on for in Army aviation. We wandered to the sleeping tent hoping tomorrow would be a better day, for us and for the guys in the mountains doing the fighting.

CHAPTER 11: LEAP OF FAITH

In flying I have learned that carelessness and overconfidence are usually far more dangerous than deliberately accepted risks.

—Wilbur Wright

27 June 2011

"WHY THE SAM HILL NOT!?" The First Sergeant was irate and glaring at me as we loaded up to begin our duty day. He was standing next to a little John Deere four-wheeled Gator that was loaded with weapons and ammo, and he wanted us to carry the cargo out to his unit in the mountains.

"Wish I could, Top, believe me I do. But we're not permitted to resupply soldiers with weapons or ammo. We're a medevac outfit, and we have to operate by Geneva Convention rules. We carry weapons and ammo and we become combatants. It's just the way it is and those are the regs."

I was hoping the mention of regulations to an old soldier might get him off my back, but it didn't work. "Look," I said pointing at the gunner's window on the side of Dustoff 7-3, "we don't even carry machineguns."

"That's ridiculous!" He stood looking around for some other way to get the badly needed gear out to his troops in the field, but we were the only game in town. Kenny Brodhead just shrugged helplessly as I dealt with the senior NCO. We could just load that stuff aboard and lower it to his soldiers on the hoist. No one would know, but we'd sworn an oath, and that meant something to those of us in the medevac business.

The First Sergeant was becoming desperate. He glanced at the equipment on his Gator and had another idea. "Look, sir—my outfit is also black on water, chow, and medical supplies. How about that stuff? Can you deliver *that*?"

"You bet we can, Top. Break out that stuff and we'll get it on board." Bringloe and Capps went to give him a hand and we pondered what was involved in a little side trip to his unit up in the Watapur. We'd have to figure a way to find his unit, somehow get the stuff bundled up, and then lowered to the ground on the hoist. No problem if that's all we had to do, but we also had to pick up two heroes—an American soldier and the ANA interpreter—plus a guy that had an infection setting into a gunshot wound.

"So, how are we gonna handle this?" I watched Capps, Bringloe and the First Sergeant loading water, rations, and delicate IV fluids onto the Blackhawk.

"How about we put it in a bodybag and lower it in that?" Capps, our resident mechanical genius had it all figured out.

"Brilliant," I said. "That's what we'll do. Y'all get a bag and wrap the load." I nodded at Kenny and we climbed in to get started while the First Sergeant gave us a grid to find his outfit. We were operating in a sort of daze. All the scared and nervous business was behind us and the entire crew functioned mostly by checklist and muscle memory. We needed to save our energy resources and brain power to handle the unexpected. The key was to just keep flying until the mission was complete. There was unlikely to be anything new to encounter after what we'd been through over the past couple of days.

I glanced out to see Bringloe and Capps standing outside the aircraft with a couple of little fire extinguishers and went on auto-pilot to get us rolling. "I've got air, fuel, and spark. Clear on one?"

"Clear!" Julia said.

I pressed the silver start button on the number one engine power control lever with my left thumb and reached up with my other hand to reset the master caution panel. We heard a reassuring series of electrical snaps that told us the ignition spark had ignited the fuel flowing into the engines. Then there was a series of high-pitched whines that merged into a roar, followed by a monkey rumble as the fuel exploded and the engines spooled up to idle. The rotors were already turning.

While we finished the engine checks, I glanced out to where Julia Bringloe was leaning on the nose of the Blackhawk. She'd been through a lot riding the hoist up and down and caring for wounded soldiers, but she didn't look concerned about heading out to do it again. Among all of us, she had the job that exposed her to the most danger. She was the one who landed down on the ground in the midst of a fight if necessary, and rode that hook dangling like a trout fly waiting for a big fish to bite. We called KIA soldiers heroes, but we had some live ones in this outfit—and Julia Bringloe was one of those. When we got the rotors turning, she whipped her ICS cable clear of the landing gear and hopped into the Blackhawk. It was just another day at the office for SGT Bringloe.

Specialist David Capps looked up at the heat waves coming off of the exhaust as Dustoff 7-3's engines warmed for flight. It was like watching a mirage on the desert sands as the Blackhawk's 1,500 shaft horsepower engines burned fuel and exhausted hot gas. He pulled the parking chocks from around the main gear and carried them into the cabin with him. "Chocks are out. Right rear is secure." He'd done it all a hundred times, and his speed left him a few moments waiting for the pilots to lift off to think about his wife and son at home. After what they'd been through over the past days, he felt more confident that he would live to see them again. He'd always done his duty—but now he was getting a lot better at it.

"Once more unto the breach, dear friends, once more…" I put my hands on the controls and squirmed into the seat. The cyclic and collective seemed to mold to my hands, and my feet felt like they were slipping into a comfortable old pair of shoes. I pressed on the pedals and released the parking brakes. I wasn't so much flying the Blackhawk as I was wearing it—all eight-and-a-half tons. If I survived this deployment and got into the flight instructor business back at Fort Rucker, I'd need to be detailed and specific about what I was doing in the cockpit—but not today. Today, I was going to fly it like I stole it.

"Ops, this is 7-3. We're off now. Catch you on the flip side."

We raced up the Kunar Valley looking at the fuel gauges. O'Brien had topped it off after a hard night policing up the last patients from the Chinook crash site. Our mission LZs were all above 8,500 feet and we'd need to burn off some fuel to get light enough for best performance at those altitudes. We made our turn and saw some Apache gunships zooming over the valley floor. Things were getting crowded up here—and there wasn't a traffic cop in sight.

"Watapur traffic, Dustoff 7-3 is inbound from south to north," Kenny advised everyone that we were coming into the area. We got an acknowledgment from an Apache making a gun-run on a target, and he provided a weather report. We still had low ceilings with banks of thick clouds higher up in the mountains.

While Kenny called the Prodigal unit that had our wounded, I took a look at the cloud cover. We were going to have to fly through the muck again, dodging cloud banks to search for our objectives. The man with the infected gunshot wound was deteriorating. The good news was that his unit was in an overwatch position and not on the move—so they'd be relatively easy to find.

"We'll do this by position priority," I said, making some quick decisions. Closest would come first. "Let's get the heroes, then deliver the supplies, and then go after the wounded. We'll have all the other stuff done at that point, and we can run the patients directly back to A'bad."

We were headed to pick up the KIAs when a message from the unit we were hauling supplies for changed our plans.

৵

"Dustoff 7-3 we have another element—Stalker 1-6—that's black on water. We need you to take care of them first. Grid to follow; prepare to copy." It was decision time again for me. We had two KIAs on the ground that needed pick-up, and now we had a unit that was out of water. The heroes would have to wait. Water was vital to the units humping down in these mountains. Without hydration, soldiers would start dropping quickly, and we'd wind up with a whole lot more missions to handle. We would deliver some water and then come back for the KIAs.

Kenny punched in the grid for Stalker 1-6 and I watched the bearing pointer swing. They were somewhere off to the left of our flight path.

"Turning left…"

"Clear left…" Bringloe told me there were no obstacles on that side, so I made the turn and checked the engines. The thirsty soldiers were at a lower altitude, which meant we'd have more power to maneuver. While Capps readied the hoist and got the water resupply ready for lowering, Kenny and I searched for the unit. We flew over the area indicated by the grid, but we couldn't see anyone on the ground. I pulled it around and went back for another pass. We still didn't see anything. We called to confirm the grid and we had it right. Either these guys weren't where they were supposed to be, or we just couldn't see them. We tried them on the radio and got nothing.

We decided to make one slower, lower pass just at treetops, hoping either we'd spot them or they would see us. As I almost brushed the trees with the belly of the aircraft, the radio came to life. "Dustoff, this is Stalker 1-6. We see you now. We're in the tree line above the LZ at your 12 o'clock."

Stomping on the right pedal to line us up, I called the ground guys. "Stalker 1-6, we need you to grab this water as quick as you can." We were fighting serious updrafts that shook the Blackhawk violently as I pulled into a hover over a clear patch of ground near the tree line.

Capps moved me around a bit as he gauged where the load had the best chance of reaching the ground intact. When he thought we had it as close as possible, he powered up the hoist and began to lower 130 pounds of vital water wrapped up in a long black bodybag. It was a weird sight. The rubber bag on the end of his hoist line looked like a big wrinkled raisin dropping into a cereal bowl.

"Hold hover," he called to me. "The bag is just about on the ground." I glanced out my window and couldn't see any kind of reception party. There was no one in sight to take charge of the load and get it off our hook. We needed to get this over with in a hurry before some Taliban RPG gunner found a juicy target of opportunity.

Suddenly, we saw a single soldier sprint out of the trees and grab the bag. He shook it like it was a dirty rug and spilled water bottles all over the LZ. When it was empty, he just tossed the bag, still attached to our cable, and scrambled around collecting water bottles. Capps let me know the bag was still attached to the hook. It was empty now and might blow around in our rotor wash like a big sail. That could be a serious problem if it came into contact with our tail rotor. I was about to tell him to start retrieving it slowly when we heard several loud, sharp cracks from somewhere near our nose.

"Taking fire; taking fire!" Kenny announced for all concerned. I instinctively yanked on the collective and shoved forward on the cyclic to get us out of there. We pulled off and climbed, looking down below for the source of the incoming rounds. We couldn't see any shooters, but at that point they were a smaller problem than what was happening in the back.

Capps was desperately struggling with the hoist cable as it raced towards our tail rotor propelled by our forward airspeed and the wind effect on the limp bodybag. He was sitting on the cabin floor with his legs dangling outside, hanging onto the hoist boom with one hand and struggling to control the cable with the other. He had no hands unoccupied that would allow him to key the ICS and let us know about the jeopardy. Bringloe quickly understood Capps had a problem and jumped across the cabin to give him a hand.

"Talk to me, guys..." But they were too busy in the back while Kenny and I just kept accelerating and clawing for altitude.

As Bringloe got to the cabin door, she could see Capps was in trouble. He was halfway out of the aircraft being buffeted hard by the wind and struggling desperately to get a firm grip on the hoist cable which was now sailing up toward our tail rotor with the empty bodybag inflated like a big, black parachute. If that bag or the steel cable contacted the tail rotor, we would promptly spin out of control and crash.

While she tried to get a grip on Capps with one hand she keyed her ICS with the other. "Stop, stop...HOLD HOVER!"

There was no questioning that. Something was seriously wrong back behind the cockpit. I pulled the cyclic into my gut and dumped the collective to the floor to stop the Blackhawk's forward progress and set up a hover. We were at 300 feet off the trees, and this was no time or place to be hanging around with enemy shooters on the ground. Bringloe was not the kind of soldier to get rattled unless it was something serious, so I made the adjustments to hold hover and waited for her to tell me what kind of trouble we had.

"The bag is heading for the tail rotor!" she said finally. "We're trying to recover it!"

There was nothing Kenny or I could do from the cockpit except hope and pray they got control of the hoist cable in a hurry. I pulled the nose up another ten degrees hoping that might help. It was the wrong move.

The tail boom lowered and nearly met the offending cable halfway as David Capps mashed the hoist control pendant's reel in button with one hand and wrestled the steel cable with the other. He was fighting what looked like a losing battle. As the aircraft decelerated to hover, the cable swung closer to the tail boom. The excess cable and the body bag snagged briefly on the stabilator wing, just under the tail rotor. He tried for more tension on the cable and watched the bag slip from under the stabilator towards the spinning blades. A couple more feet and it would get caught in the tail rotor, destroying it instantly.

Capps dropped the pendant and kicked out with his legs trying to get one hooked over the cable. His monkey-strap was all that was holding him to the bucking aircraft. He kicked and missed and then kicked again, inching ever farther outside the helicopter. He saw the bodybag whipping in the wind, nearly free of the stabilator wing and made one last desperate effort to hook the cable with his legs. That one worked. He jerked back with his legs and got some slack in the cable that allowed him to get his hands on it. He had a modicum of control now and managed to pull the bodybag away from the tail rotor. Holding on to his purchase with all his strength, he fought to get his body back inside 9-4-4, where he'd have better leverage to pull.

Bringloe wrapped her arms around him and fell backward pulling him inside. While she helped him wrestle the cable, Capps activated the reel-in button on the hoist for highest speed recovery. The crisis was past as they sat panting near the door and watched the cable spool back into the reel. When the flapping black bodybag that had nearly wrecked their ride was snagged on the cabin door handle, Capps just shook his head and leaned back outside to get it. Specialist David Capp had saved our lives.

"We're clear. Go!" Julia Bringloe ordered in a nearly breathless croak. It was a while before we got a full report from her and Capps on what had happened and what they did to save us all. As they related the details, vastly understating David's heroic efforts, Kenny and I just listened, steering

Dustoff 7-3 toward the next pick-up site and wondering how we got lucky enough to have soldiers like David Capps and Julia Bringloe on our crew.

CHAPTER 12: THE HERO

**Greater love hath no man than this,
that a man lay down his life for his friends.**

—John 15:13

27 June 2011

THERE WAS STILL A LOT OF missions to fly and the next challenge involved some other heroes. We were scheduled to pick-up an ANA Interpreter and an American that had both been killed in action around the disputed *qalat*, the fortified village that had been giving units in the area a very difficult time. The platoon had already suffered an 80 percent casualty rate. We were all quite familiar with that spot because that's where Dustoff 7-2 nearly got shot out of the air, where we almost died during the precarious one-wheel the night before. The bad guys were still holding ground around there and resisting all effort to pry them out of it.

That was one bad thing. The other was that the KIAs had to be lifted in bodybags, and none of us wanted a repeat tussle with one of those things flapping in the wind. Of course, if we did it right, Julia would carry the bags down in a roll and they would come up under the weight of the dead bodies, so we thought we'd be OK. Bringloe would ride down and load up a body. Capps would get it and then retrieve Julia. Then it was on to the next one. There was a flight of Apache gunships working over the area to cover us. Other than the impenetrable weather, what could go wrong?

Kenny and I followed the GPS toward the *qalat*. We could see a number of vicious firefights going on as we traversed the area, surfing along the steep cliffs and trying to come up with a plan if the weather got any worse. It was closing fast all over the area and we might encounter Inadvertent Instrument Meteorological Conditions or just IIMC for short. What that means in real people talk is that the aircrew suddenly finds itself blinded by weather and unable to see where they're going. In that case you went IFR or Instrument Flight Rules and headed for someplace that had an ILS or Instrument Landing System to guide you back onto the ground. Bagram had an ILS, but if we had to divert after our pick-up, we'd need enough fuel, so I did some quick calculations as Kenny steered us through the soup toward our objective.

Bagram Air Base was about 30 minutes flying time from the Watapur Valley, so we'd need sufficient juice to get us there with the added weight of two dead men plus the rations and medical gear we still needed to deliver and maybe make a couple of approaches before we got it on the ground. My shaky math indicated we could do it with the fuel we had— but just barely. We hoped for improving weather and flew where the GPS told us to go. There was an outfit up ahead, holding the KIAs and waiting for them to be hauled off the battlefield. Until we took the heroes off their hands, Prodigal 1-7 and the rest of 1st Platoon were stuck and unable to move an inch.

The weather was really getting ugly by the time we got into contact with the ground. They were ready for us, but we couldn't see much down below through blowing clouds and a heavy mist. It looked like Victorian London in an old Sherlock Holmes movie. When we were five minutes out from the designated pick-up site, I called the Apaches to let them know we were coming into the area. We could hear the pilots talking to the ground units as they rattled over the *qalat* looking for targets.

"Dustoff, this is Joker 4-3, we have you in sight. We'll cover you into the LZ," an Apache gunship pilot responded. "Be advised you've got a thick cloud layer dropping down from above. Expect we'll lose visual on you."

OK—our fire support from the air was unlikely to see us when we went into the zone. And once we disappeared, they'd be holding back for fear of hitting us if they tried to suppress any ground fire we might take. I just glanced at Kenny who was thinking the same black thoughts and then told Capps and Bringloe to get ready. We needed to get this thing done. The outfit on the ground with the KIAs was stuck. Their proposed reinforcements had been shot out of the game in the Chinook crash.

"Power to the hoist," Kenny said, flipping the switches as I brought us over the designated spot. It was gusty near the *qalat* which I could just see off to my right. I had to do a little tap dance on the pedals to keep us pointed in the right direction facing south while Bringloe grabbed a rolled up bodybag and moved to mount the hook. She was getting strapped in when the radios erupted with excited transmissions from ground forces engaging a heavy enemy attack off to our east. She got rattled listening to it, and unplugged from the ICS. Staying abreast of what was happening in the fight was a distraction from what she needed to do.

Capps rolled open the door and boomed the hoist out into the scorching air. It felt like a hair dryer on high, blasting his face. Then he sat on the cabin floor with his legs dangling, pressing the switch to lower Bringloe. We needed to avoid drifting, so he looked around for something that might keep me oriented as I flew from the blind side. "Come forward...three... two...one...and hold hover. You see that tree, sir?"

There were a lot of trees in the area, but I judged I could see the one he meant—a tall pine that looked to be stretched up about a hundred feet off the ground. "I've got it, Capps." I stared at the mark and put my chin bubble about two feet away from the top branches. We just hung there like a Christmas ornament while Bringloe headed for the ground. There wasn't much else for me to do except focus on the tree and make deft little adjustments to hold the hover. Kenny was on the uphill side where the enemy was last reported to be, and he'd let me know in a hurry if he saw muzzle flashes. As usual at this point in a mission, it was all up to the boy and girl in back.

As she slowly spun down to the ground, SGT Bringloe spotted the *qalat* and some soldiers lying prone on the ground below her. When she touched down and climbed off the hook, two men ran out from the trees carrying the body of the dead ANA interpreter. He was fairly ripe having been killed three days earlier, but they ignored the smell and struggled to get the stiffened body into the bag. They were just getting it all hooked up for lift when there was a wicked burst of incoming fire that tore up the ground around them. Her helpers dove for cover, but Bringloe ignored it and kept working to get the bodybag secured to the hoist cable.

"You might want to lay down with us!" A soldier grabbed her by the arm and pulled her into cover as his buddies opened up on the shooters. The little close-in firefight went on for a few moments and then devolved into a few desultory shots. Julia scanned to see if it was clear, then ran back into the open. All around her, the grunts just shook their heads. These medevac people were gutsy—and a little bit crazy. Bringloe got the bodybag secured, looked up at Capps to give him a thumbs-up, and then ran back to dive into cover beside the soldiers.

"I've got the hero—cabling up," Capps reported in calm tones. We had ground fire down below but none of it seemed to be aimed directly at us. That might not last much longer, so I focused and silently went through the 46th Psalm to calm myself. Kenny was watching everything that didn't directly involve holding this hover. If I took a round, he'd be on the controls immediately. *Just hold this hover,* I told myself, *and do what needs to be done. Everything else is in God's hands.*

"Load is at the cabin." Capps had the bodybag within reach. Now he'd just drag it inside and recover Julia and we'd be mission complete on this one. That was the good news—but Capps related the bad news shortly thereafter.

"I got a problem," he said. "I can't lift him!"

Capps was struggling with what felt like a load of heavy bricks as he strained and reached for a better grip on the bag containing the dead Terp. The body had shifted during the lift and now hung nearly vertical below the aircraft. Capps had to grab at an end and haul nearly 200 pounds of dead weight straight up until he got enough of it inside the aircraft to get him some leverage. He was in good shape, but he was no weightlifter at a skinny 140 pounds. To complicate matters, the body had begun to decompose making him gag at the foul odor that was blown into the cabin by the updraft of our rotor wash. He needed help—but there was nobody else in the cabin.

"Can you run the hoist for me and get him a little closer?"

"You got it." Kenny said and reached for the remote controls. It was a new one on me. I'd never heard of a combat hoist being run by pilots in the cockpit. That was only an emergency drill—something you did in training mainly just to demonstrate it could be done. Now we were going to do it for real. Without a visual clue about what was happening in the cabin or on the ground below, Kenny was going to manipulate the controls and try to bring the hoist into the cabin as soon as Capps managed to get the body high enough to make room. He strained his neck as far as it would turn to try and catch a glimpse of Capps to help him. I got back to hovering and praying while they worked it out.

In the back of Dustoff 7-3, Capps swallowed bile and wrapped his arms around the foul-smelling bundle that refused to clear the door. He bear-hugged the bag and flexed his legs, lifting with all his might. He got it a few inches higher, but not enough to clear the deck so Brodhead could bring it inside the helicopter. When he couldn't hang on anymore, Capps let the load slip and the bodybag dropped a few feet. We were hovering over a firefight and he didn't have the strength to get his part of the job done.

Kenny craned further over his seat and tried to see what was happening in the back. The fight on the ground was getting hotter and we had to get on with this deal.

"Capps, Capps!" Kenny shouted. "Listen to me, man! This is it, Capps. This is your moment! Adrenaline, brother—give it everything you've got!"

Capps heard the encouraging words in his headset and reached for the corpse again, clasping it tightly. With Kenny Brodhead cheering him on, he lifted with strength he didn't know he had. His blood was boiling and he was grunting with the strain—but the body was finally moving. He staggered back, pulling hard with his arms and legs as more of the load came clear of the door.

"Booming in!" Kenny Brodhead gave a triumphant whoop and hit the controls to bring the boom and the load inside the Blackhawk. He collapsed back into his seat chuckling as he congratulated Capps. "Great job, David! You the man, brother. You the man!"

Capps was collapsed on the floor of the cabin, pinned underneath the bodybag he'd just hauled aboard. It was even ranker in the confines of the cabin. He choked and scrambled to get out from under the weight. When he finally stopped shaking, he took a deep breath and hauled the hero away from the door. He still needed to retrieve Bringloe. Capps placed his right hand on the floor and side-vaulted over the hero, plopping back down on the edge of the aircraft.

"Booming out!" Capps said. We could hear him panting with exertion but he seemed to be focused and ready for the next step. David Capps was turning into a beast of a crew chief.

⁂

Sergeant Julia Bringloe had watched her crewmate's struggle from a covered position on the ground. She saw the bodybag disappear and the boom come back out ready for lift and shouted to the soldiers who were watching for the nearby shooters to open up again. It was quiet, but everyone knew what that meant. The shooters were waiting for a suitable target. If they waited, they'd acquire an easy kill without having to expose themselves to counter-fire from the American soldiers.

"Give me three-sixty security!" Bringloe shouted and ran toward the hook that was dropping onto the ground in open terrain. As she straddled the JP and snapped on her safety lines, she looked around at the exhausted soldiers all staring back at her as she began to rise and present the enemy shooters with a prime aiming point. Some of them looked as if they couldn't believe what they were seeing. Others looked like they envied the female soldier about to get out of this mess. It was all the same to Bringloe rising toward the hovering Blackhawk. She was one of them and she shared the risks.

∽

About 100 meters uphill from the spot where Julia Bringloe hung below the helicopter, six Taliban fighters rose cautiously and aimed in on her with AK-47s. When they could see her plainly as a silhouette against the trees, they pressed their triggers and opened fire.

∽

"She's coming up. They're shooting at her!" Capps reported the situation about the same time we got similar word from the ground guys.

"Dustoff, be advised your medic is under fire." I resisted the impulse to just pull pitch and get out of the area. Julia was still below the treetops and dragging her through that mess might kill her. Kenny Brodhead saw muzzle flashes on his side, reached for the M-4 carbine racked near the center console and chambered a round. He searched in vain for a clear shot.

I struggled to hold the hover and shouted for Capps to give me a progress report. We continued to take fire for the next ten seconds, but all of it was aimed at Julia on the hoist. The bad guys wanted to shoot the sitting duck and they knew from hard experience if they raised their aim and started shooting at us, the Apaches would drill into them like buzz-saws. The gunships were still out there looking for targets to shoot, daring the bad guys to show themselves. One of them came up on the radio and said "Dustoff, you guys are crazy!" That was understandable—and also wrong. We weren't insane, reckless, or some sort of lunatic adrenaline junkies. We just seemed to get ourselves into situations where we had no choice other than to do something crazy. And this was one of those situations.

Julia could hear the green tracers that were whistling by on either side of her as she still hung 50 feet below our Blackhawk. Capps knew it wouldn't be long before one of the better shooters hit her. He could continue reeling her in while we were on the move out of the line of fire.

"Go, go, go!"

And that's what we did with great speed and relish. I dropped the nose and pulled in all the power the engines could safely generate. With Bringloe dangling and slowly rising toward the safety of our cabin, we shot up to the floor of the clouds like a rocket. There had been a lot of ground fire, and I scanned the instruments to see if any of it had hit us or done significant damage. The status panels all said we were OK, so I inquired about our dangling flight medic.

"She's at the door. Booming in!" Capps reached out and grabbed Julia's hands to pull her into the cabin. They both collapsed on the floor staring at each other with that funny expression—a mix of terror and elation—like survivors of near-fatal car crashes.

We rocketed down the hillside and skirted below the soup as I turned us onto a southerly heading for A'bad. On the valley floor below us, there was a bunch of local kids enjoying a beautiful day, playing soccer, oblivious to the war up in the mountains or to the eight-ton helicopter rattling overhead with a dead countryman aboard.

CHAPTER 13: BLIND FAITH

Do the thing you fear most and the death of fear is certain.

—Mark Twain

27 June 2011

IT WAS A LONG TRIP through worsening weather back to A'bad. Kenny and I kept running checks of vital systems. It seemed impossible that none of the shooters on the ground had managed to hit us with all the rounds that were being exchanged. Bringloe had a few close ones as she rode the cable, but none hit her despite the bad guys' best efforts.

She sat in the back staring at the dead ANA soldier decomposing in the bodybag and tried not to think about the close call. She'd survived, and if her lucky streak held, she'd live to see her son waiting with family back in Hawaii. And what she'd done recovering the dead man was important. With that burden off their hands, the infantry guys might be able to get moving and wipe out some of those stubborn shooters around the *qalat*. No doubt she would have to go back to that place and yo-yo up and down again before the day was done. She liked to think the grunts would forge ahead and maybe make it a little safer for her. She slumped in her seat and reached into the pocket of her flight suit for a handful of grimy Gummy Bears.

"A'bad Control, Dustoff 7-3 is inbound from the north with a hero and refuel." Kenny announced our arrival as I set up the approach. Looking down at the party waiting for us, I was hoping to see some ANA soldiers with their national colors flying to retrieve their dead countrymen with appropriate respect. The only thing I saw was a party of U.S. Army medics waiting to retrieve the bodybag. What happened after that was anybody's guess, but I presumed he would be turned over to the man's command or family.

There were no formalities or salutes on the ground. There wasn't even time to shut down. When the medics had the bodybag off-loaded, several soldiers walked up carrying a couple more bags loaded with water and IV fluids. We were going to do some more resupply and another hero pickup, as well as handle any remaining medevacs up in the mountains. That made us heavy, and there was no telling how much anybody we picked up might weigh. The mountains were high, the weather was bad, the helicopter was tired—and so were we. It was time for some more calculations to decide how much fuel we needed to get at the FARP.

If we got too little, we'd run out of gas up in the valley. Not a good option. If we took too much, we'd have trouble climbing and maneuvering at the required altitudes. As we waited for a slot at the FARP at A'bad, I scanned the gauges. We had just a splash of fuel aboard and we'd been burning about 1,000-pounds-an-hour so far. The current nine-line concerning the wounded man we were scheduled to retrieve said he was waiting at a location about 10,500 feet up on one of the mountainsides. Temperatures up there ran about 77 degrees Fahrenheit, which was going to put a strain on our engines and burn more fuel. Add to that a deteriorating weather situation which might cause us to go on instruments and divert to Bagram, and things got complicated. We needed enough but not too much and the margins were paper-thin.

By the time our turn at the FARP came and the fuel crews had us hooked up, I finished the figures. "Uh, Kenny?"

"Yeah, what's up?" He glanced across the cockpit alerted by the sound of my voice. "We got a problem?"

"It's like this..." I ran through the situation for him. "Max torque available is eighty-four percent and we'll need all of that to hold hover at designated altitude. We get heavy and have to pull more power up there—we fall out of the sky and die."

"Don't want that..."

"No. So we can take eight-hundred pounds of gas and that's it."

Julia had been monitoring the conversation and added her concerns. "The nine-line says the unit is in contact, so they probably can't move him down the mountain to a lower attitude, and he's got a few bullet holes so he's probably not real mobile anyway."

"I like it..." Capps was the only one that seemed unconcerned. "Let's do it."

I called back to have the crew stop our fuel flow. We either had it right or we didn't. I started to second guess myself, but I was pretty sure Kenny had double-checked it in his head. He was saying nothing though, and I appreciated his vote of confidence as we steered clear of the FARP and turned toward the cloudbank that was rolling toward us from the mouth of the valley.

"A'bad traffic, Dustoff 7-3 is sliding right out of point one in the FARP. We're departure to the north for patient pick-up."

Sergeant Reyes came up on the net with a weather report and it wasn't encouraging. "Dustoff 7-3, be advised you're heading into the soup. Apaches in the area are reporting the LZ is completely socked in. How copy?"

"Copy all, Ops. We're gonna give it a try. See you later."
Kenny took the controls and maneuvered in a snaky path up the Kunar Valley, looking for our turn into the Watapur where our patient waited. The mountains looked like crumpled paper bags tossed randomly into the area. At lower elevations, they were mottled with brown and green, but up high—up at the elevations we needed to reach—the peaks were shrouded in thick grey clouds. The sun shone brightly over the valley floor, but up higher those clouds cast dark ominous shadows. Visibility would be somewhere between a joke and nonexistent.

It was increasingly skosh as we made our turn into the Watapur. "So that's where we're going, kids."

"Uh, yeah, OK." Capps sounded a little less confident than he had back at the FARP.

"Watapur traffic, Dustoff 7-3 is ingress from the south to the east ridgeline for patient pickup." Kenny let any pilot flying near this mess know that we had joined the party, and then switched frequencies to let the ground unit know we were on our way. "Cherokee 6, Dustoff 7-3 is inbound your location for patient pick-up. We'll call two minutes out for you to mark the LZ."

"Dustoff, this is Cherokee 6—roger. Be advised we have enemy in the area and we are out of smoke."

We acknowledged as we rose into the dense clouds, but it didn't look like it was going to make much difference. Even if they had smoke to pop for us, we probably couldn't see it. An Apache pilot called as we drove deeper into the soup and let us know we were no longer in sight. They had enough sense to stay out of the fog.

"Roger Cherokee. Can you see the sky from your position?"

"Yeah, a little bit. I think you'll be fine to make it in here." At least the infantry was confident. They could see the sky "a little bit," but we could barely see the ground as we slithered through little holes in the blowing cloud-cover. We were straining to see through the clouds, and every once in a while someone reported they caught a patch of steep hillside. When that happened, we adjusted course to keep plenty of room between the slope and our rotor disk. If we blew it and flew into something solid and rode it into the ground, that wounded soldier on the ground would be suffering for a long time before someone else came to the rescue.

"All right, Cherokee. We'll find a way to get to you. Stand by." I tried to keep my voice light and confident with a hint of humor. Façade of confidence. Bringloe and Capps reported they were all set in the back as soon as we found the ground and located our patient on it.

"This is nuts, Kenny." I looked over to see him grinning, showing some teeth below that enviable mustache. We'd both heard stories about Dustoff crews in Vietnam trying similar stunts when impenetrable mists rose to hide wounded men in the jungle-covered mountains. Way too many of those tales ended up with fiery crashes.

"Well, at least the bad guys can't see us…" In the cockpit, the glass was rarely half-empty with Kenny Brodhead—it was just filled to half of its potential.

We found a little channel in the clouds and Kenny steered us into it, following a slow path to the right toward where the clouds looked a little lighter. He flew us cautiously through the channel, still climbing until we finally popped up into a clearer patch. On our right was a long, jagged ridge-line covered with tall pines. Clouds drifted past the area running from north to south, but at least we had a flimsy orientation to the ground. Behind us now was a solid wall of thick cloud. We were in the area approximately where we needed to be, but it put us in the only clear air available. We were surrounded on every other side by walls of white. The GPS said we were in the grid, so I contacted the ground unit.

"Cherokee 6, we are short final for your location. Searching now."

We weren't the only ones searching for some kind of marker. Bringloe and Capps were hanging out of the cabin like trapeze artists and sweeping the area for clues.

"I got nothing on this side." Capps was clueless. "I can't see a thing."

"No joy left rear."

Kenny pointed at the GPS. The indicator was swinging to indicate the location we wanted was now to our rear. We'd passed right over them. He edged us slowly and carefully ahead keeping a close eye on the cliffs, but there was still nothing in sight. The infantry had no smoke, there was no way to see a panel on the ground, and we were surrounded by a fogbank. There had to be a better way.

"Turn back and head south again and run the ridgeline. I've got an idea." As we motored back in the opposite direction, I called the ground unit.

"Cherokee 6, this is Dustoff. We're going to run the ridgeline north to south. When you start to hear us, count down from five to one until we're directly over you. How copy?"

"Roger, Dustoff. Got it!"

"Good idea, Erik. Hope it works." Kenny maneuvered us as slowly as he could back along the ridgeline. At this ultra-slow speed at high altitude, power demand on the engines increased and there was a distinct possibility of overheat and rotor droop. I kept my eyes on the gauges. Kenny needed to focus on flying, so I'd watch everything else for him. In the back, Capps got the boom deployed and Bringloe mounted the hook. If the soldiers found us or we found them, they wanted to be quick off the mark.

"Dustoff we hear you in five...four...three...two...one. You're right over the top of us now!"

"I got 'em; I got 'em!" Capps shouted, and Kenny said he could also see something on the ground. Looking down through the chin bubble, I spotted a couple of soldiers in camouflage darting through the trees off our nose. Kenny established a hover in gusty winds and checked his available power.

"Max torque is eighty-four percent, right? How we doing?"

"You're at eighty-two percent, Kenny." We were cutting it thin. Any power adjustments that forced much more torque, and the rotors would stop spinning. The key was to get this thing done in a hurry while we were within the safe-operating envelope.

"Cherokee, this is Dustoff. We're sending down our medic to get your wounded man. Then we're gonna send your resupply. At that point, we'll lift your wounded man and our medic. This has to happen very, very fast. Do you understand that?"

"Roger, copy very, very fast..."

"Medic's on the ground," Capps had Julia down and she was sprinting uphill for the treeline to retrieve the wounded soldier. "I'm gonna send down the supplies."

Kenny held us at 100 feet above the little clearing while I watched the gauges and prayed for speed from all involved. The longer we hung out up here, the more likely the engines would decide they'd had enough and stop cooperating. There was nothing to see outside the cockpit, so I craned over my seat back and caught a glimpse of Capps struggling to get two bulky bodybags full of water and IV fluids hooked up for descent on the hoist. When he had the load descending, I sat back and took a look in the other direction outside our windscreens and up through the greenhouse. The clouds were getting thicker and closer with every second. It was as if we were being swallowed up on all sides by a tsunami of fog. Inside the aircraft, the surfaces took on a ghostly glow as we were consumed by the mist.

"Cherokee, your water and meds are on the way. Grab them and run. We're gonna throw the rations down, so heads up."

Capps could see the soldiers trying to comply. They were grabbing at the water and medical supplies and running with armloads back to the trees. "They got the stuff and the bags. I'm cabling up now."

Kenny cut a glance outside his window at the encroaching wall of grey. "OK, I'm starting to lose some visuals over here, Erik." He cut his eyes back inside and watched the vertical situation indicator. He needed to keep it steady and avoid drifting until we got the rations dumped and recovered Bringloe. The seconds seemed like hours and the grin was gone from Kenny's face.

"Cable's up. I'm tossing the MREs. Bomb's away!" Capps was heaving 20-pound ration boxes out of the cabin as fast as he could. Most of them didn't survive the fall intact. Boxes hit the ground and exploded like piñatas strewing plastic ration bags all over the hillside. Hungry soldiers who hadn't eaten for some time were scrambling to retrieve them like a bunch of kids on an Easter egg hunt.

"I'm gonna brain somebody in a minute." Capps was trying to keep from dropping one of the heavy boxes on the scrambling soldiers but they were paying no attention to his problems as they scampered back and forth under the air-craft. "There's guys are everywhere down there. I can't find a clear spot."

"Just throw it as far away as you can," I told him. "We don't have time…"

Capps aimed away from the clustered soldiers and heaved the last two ration boxes clear of the aircraft. He spotted Bringloe churning out of the trees with her casualty and all his gear.

"Medic is inbound. She's got the patient and his gear. Booming out."

As the hook descended for Bringloe and our medevac, I checked the power. We were doing better at 80 percent of torque, though it was bouncing up and down quite a bit. We might just get away with this, but we still had to find a way out of the soup.

"I can see some treetops on my side, Kenny. We might be able to egress over to my side." All I saw was the very top of three trees. I looked across the cockpit and saw my friend was under a serious strain. He was facing a lot of equally bad options.

"You OK?"

"I got it. But it's getting blurry real quick." Kenny Brod-head was not about to give up, but he wanted me to know his situation and I appreciated the honesty. I checked my watch and studiously avoided yelling for a progress report from the back. They knew their business back there. Capps and Bringloe would not be idling while we were teetering on the edge of serious trouble.

Bringloe dropped the big black man with the gunshot wounds and piled his equipment next to the hook. He was maybe 250 pounds and his ruck and gear weighed another 70 for about 320 on the hook plus her weight. *Why don't I ever get the small guys*, she wondered as she got him hooked up to the JP and slung his ruck over a shoulder.

"This is going to be fun," she said and showed Capps a thumbs-up. As they lifted off the ground on the straining hoist-line, she looked up and saw the helicopter disappear. Clouds drifted in below the Blackhawk and she lost depth perception. They were on their way up, but she had no way to gauge progress. She could tell the hoist had gone into low gear winching speed under the weight and was slowing down automatically to handle the strain. She got a little better grip on the wounded man, hoping she wasn't in for another dangling ride through the treetops.

"Medic and patient are off the ground," Capps said. The added weight caused Kenny to call for more power from the engines. The gauge was showing right at max allowable torque.

"Eighty-three percent torque, Kenny." I tried to make it sound like an off-hand reminder that we were in the danger zone, but I could see him glance over to confirm my reading. Rivulets of sweat were running down his cheeks. This was dicey in the extreme. Any tiny control input that brought on more torque, even a half-inch, and we'd droop the rotors. We'd slam Julia, patient, helicopter, and crew into the ground and hope for the best while the rotors chewed us all apart. Our only options were steady, professional performance, reliable engines, and prayer.

"Still showing eighty-three percent. Rotors good," I said as much to reassure myself as Kenny.

Julia looked up and saw something—the most beautiful thing she had ever seen. The rotor blades were slicing into a thick layer of cloud that was collapsing on us. We had created a low pressure system, a bubble of clearness. As the moist air recirculated upwards, it caught the sunlight. Surrounding her in every direction was the most brilliant rainbow. The aircraft had disappeared into an incredible display of color—and the whole world became frighteningly silent.

"I can't see Sergeant Bringloe anymore!" Capps shouted from the cabin and I looked out to see that clouds had slipped in under the aircraft. The hillside we'd been using for orientation was also gone. We were in a big white soup bowl. Once we lost visual references, we had to start an immediate climb or we risked drifting into the mountain. That would take power and we had none to spare. I ran through the options in seconds. We needed to accelerate and trade airspeed for altitude, but if we did that, we might drag Julia and her patient through the trees or hit some piece of ground we couldn't see below us. Our best bet was to turn to what looked like the clear side before the fog folded in on us and inch away from the mountain with an eye on the GPS distance counter and the vertical speed indicator to make sure we weren't sinking. Meanwhile, Julia and her patient would get another long, dangling ride until the hoist finally brought them up to safety.

"Erik, I've lost visual references, committing to IMC!" Kenny said.

"Roger, we're inadvertent!" I called back to Kenny and called any other traffic in the area to let them know we were about to fly away from the hillside completely blind. "Watapur traffic, Watapur traffic, Dustoff 7-3 is punching in inadvertent IMC on the east side of the valley, heading 2-0-0, climbing to 14,000 feet. We'll be en route Bagram."

On the hook below Dustoff 7-3, Julia Bringloe sensed the movement as the hoist cable began to sway. She understood from experience what was happening with her crewmates up above in the Blackhawk. They were punching into the soup, trying to get away from the hillside, and flying out of their predicament on instruments. She was in for another ride on the cable. "Hang on!" She yelled in her patient's ear. "They're gonna fly away!"

The soldier just hugged her tightly, hiding his head on her shoulder as they soared through thick wet clouds with no orientation up, down, or sideways. It was like trying to water ski through a big vat of cottage cheese. Gone was the deafening sound of the helicopter, replaced by a screeching howl of thick clouds that screamed past her. It was disorienting and frightening, but Julia Bringloe came to peace with it. *Am I already dead?* she thought. The cable was suspended by nothing, floating with her patient silently. She was at peace. She would live or die in the next few seconds. That was in God's hands, and in the hands of the three men up above in the Blackhawk that were doing everything in their power to save her and her patient.

"I've got power," Kenny said and focused on the instruments. "Turning to a heading of 2-0-0…accelerating…"

With my hands gripping holds to keep them well away from the controls, I called our progress so Kenny could keep his mind on the instruments. "Eighty-three percent torque, five knots—eighty-three and ten—fifteen knots. We're through ETL." We passed through Effective Translational Lift, the turbulent air that a helicopter experiences as it switches to forward flight. That was progress. We were very slowly gaining speed and moving into clearer, smoother sky. We could climb a bit now without asking for dangerous levels of power. We took our first breath.

I pointed to the charts we'd laid out earlier when we were considering a possible divert for weather and then checked the Electronic Data Manager that gave us an idea of other air traffic in the area. "We've got the instrument approach data for Bagram and the EDM shows no traffic in our path. We're only gonna have enough fuel to make one attempt at landing before we run out of gas, Kenny." We still had Bringloe and a patient hanging below us in the clouds.

"No joy," Capps reported. "They're still cabling up. Counter reads seventy feet below...sixty feet below..." I told him to keep us advised and prayed that our maneuver hadn't caused her to hit the ground or slam into yet another tree as we fought through the turbulence trying to get clear of the mountainside. The altimeter showed we were climbing. At 11,000 feet, we got another piece of good news.

"I see her," Capps shouted. He looked down through the clouds to see Julia Bringloe appear looking up at him and wearing a huge grin with wet vapors running down her dirty face. Her patient was also craning his neck to look up and hanging onto Bringloe like a kid hugging a favorite teddy bear, his face white as a ghost.

"Medic's at the door. Booming in."

"Is she OK?"

"She's fine," Capps responded with a laugh. "And so is the patient. Door's closed."

Bringloe unstrapped and got her patient laid out in the cabin where she could check his vitals and repair any damage done by the wild ride. When he was stable and as comfortable as she could make him, she collapsed into her seat and just shook her head. In a few moments she and Capps were both laughing.

We had averted a couple of crises, but we still had to get the aircraft and patient safely on the ground. Even though it was further away, in this weather, Bagram Air Base was the only option. It would be a while before we got back to FOB Joyce, if we could even get back at all. I punched up the satellite comm frequency and called Johnny Reyes to let them know they probably shouldn't wait up for us.

"Ops, this is 7-3. We have the patient. We are IMC at this time, headed to Bagram. Call ahead and let them know. We'll be fuel critical when we arrive on station."

Below us, as I fiddled with the radios, I spotted a brief snatch of brown desert and a sliver of silver shining off the Pech River valley in the sunlight. It was what instrument fliers called a "sucker hole," an opening in dense cloud cover through which you could see the ground. The temptation was always to dive for the clear spot and get through the soup, but it was often a sucker move. You might fly clear through that hole—or it might swallow you up and you'd just get more lost and hit the ground.

"Kenny, sucker hole at ten o'clock low."

"Awesome. Let's give it a shot." Kenny's glass was half-full as always. He called for clearance to turn left and descend and got it from the crew in back. Our nose fell, and we rocketed down through a narrowing tunnel in the clouds. The sucker bet paid off and we broke through into clear air over the Pech River Valley with the water glinting in dim sunlight, just as the hole behind us closed up as quickly as it had appeared. Kenny grinned; mopped at his mustache, and turned us toward A'bad while I called Reyes to let him know our plans had changed. We were hitting all the lucky strokes today.

"Ops, Dustoff 7-3—we found a way through the soup. We're inbound A'bad. We'll deliver the patient and refuel. Then RTB. See you soonest."

CHAPTER 14: STAND DOWN

My religious belief teaches me to feel as safe in battle as in bed. God has fixed the time for my death. I do not concern myself about that, but to be always ready, no matter when it may overtake me. That is the way all men should live, and then all would be equally brave.
—General Thomas "Stonewall" Jackson

27 June 2011

THERE WAS A LOT of silence on the ICS as we chugged through fair visibility back toward A'bad. Each of us was pondering what we just went through, the close calls and the great escape we'd finally managed to make. Much of it was so overwhelming that it was hard to explain or express. We were completely wrung-out—mentally and physically exhausted by the constant strain. We mumbled inanities and reminded each other that we'd worked well together, saved some lives, and got a difficult job done.

Kenny and Capps told Julia what a great job she'd done. I added my compliments and said something similar to Kenny and Capps. By this time, they all knew how much I loved and respected them, but it's hard to put that kind of thing in soldierly words flying over Afghanistan in a banged-up helicopter.

We chugged into Joyce and got Dustoff 7-3 on the ground, going through the shutdown like zombies. I stood on the pad itching in all kinds of hot-spots and smelling rank in a salt-stained flight suit, watching Kenny, Bringloe, and

Capps unload their gear like they were lifting bags full of bowling balls. The adrenaline rush only lasts long enough to get you through the short run. For the long run, we were wiped out, and even minor chores seemed both overwhelming and irritating. We needed to rest for more than a few hours, and it was up to me as pilot-in-command to see that we all got it.

ᴘ

As we ambled toward ops, I thanked God for deliverance and asked for the strength to do what had to be done now. We walked into the building and drew some wide-eyed stares from the ops soldiers and the relief crew. Kenny, Bringloe, and Capps dropped their gear and just stood there staring into the distance. I headed over to check in with SGT Reyes as curious people began to ask what happened out in the Watapur.

Capps was the only one that seemed willing to respond, but he was young and still feeling a little of the rush. "We punched in IMC with Sergeant Brinlgoe still on the hoist." He looked around as his audience turned their attention to Julia Bringloe who just shrugged and went to find a soda in the break room.

Reyes had an understanding look on his face as I stood slumped before his desk. "Weather had got the valley socked in. Most of the other aircraft are waiting for it to clear. Word is that the grunts are finally moving now. It should be over before too much longer."

"Any other missions for us?"

"Nada," he said. "Captain Wilson said to give him a call as soon as you guys landed."

That could wait for a minute. I walked over to where Kenny, Bringloe, and Capps were all slumped against some stretchers. I needed to assess our condition before I talked to the commander.

"Folks, I know you've been through a lot. How're you doing?"

Kenny Brodhead just shrugged and sipped at his Diet Coke. He would go if I did.

Capps and Bringloe looked like they were waiting for me to tell them we had another mission to fly. They glared at me for a moment and then their expressions softened.

"I'm OK..." Julia Bringloe looked at her hands and picked at a broken fingernail.

"I'm good," David Capps said rubbing at an aching neck. "Let's go."

I looked at them trying to communicate with my eyes what I couldn't find the words to say. And then I just shook my head and went over to sit silently next to Kenny, joining him in staring at the floor.

They were lying to me for the finest possible reasons. They were soldiers and they would fight their way through the exhaustion, frustration, and whatever else duty demanded, but they all knew that pushing any further was suicide. That was a personal concern and it came after concerns with duties as demanded. The duty was flying and saving lives and the risks involved came with it. Terry and his crew were still here, as was 9-4-4. I had a tough call to make.

I was done and I knew it. It had been a weekend to remember: one for the times when veterans gathered to tell war stories. It had been an exhausting couple of days that was so full of close calls that it was hard to remember the routine parts of it. I looked at Kenny Brodhead over the rim of the soda can with a question in my eyes.

"Erik," he said with a sigh, "I think we're done."

It was time to find a phone. I got hold of 4ᵗʰ Platoon command post at J'Bad and slumped into a chair feeling the aches in my knees and back. I asked for CPT Wilson and tried to decide what I would say while I waited for him to get on the line.

"Hey, Sir. It's Sabiston up at A'bad..."

"Sabby! What's going on? How are you guys holding up?"

"We're OK; down and safe at Joyce. We just went IIMC on the last hoist." I paused to think and then just let it come. "My crew is done, sir. We need to stand down." I don't know what I was expecting after telling my commander that we couldn't safely carry on with the mission, but what I heard surprised me.

"Dude, I've been waiting for you guys to say the word," Captain Wilson said. "Listen, you've done some amazing things up there. We've been watching you the whole time. Stand down, Brother. We'll get you back here on a flight as soon as the weather clears. We got a replacement crew from Bagram and we'll send a fresh one to swap out with yours. Good job, man!"

With thanks for his understanding, I hung up on CPT Wilson at J'bad and strolled over to take a look at the situation maps. Units were moving all over the cloud-covered mountains up in the Watapur Valley, and the little markers showing enemy concentrations were decreasing. Taliban and Al Qaeda forces were starting to run out of ammunition and people and there were reports that the disputed *qalat* was now secure. The status board showing the number of killed and wounded was fairly static. I knew we'd saved some of those wounded soldiers in the flying we'd done. Through it all, we'd only lost one Dustoff bird to enemy action and that one would likely fly again before long. We'd all been scared, but that was combat SOP. None of us had been seriously wounded or killed. Call it a job well done and another mission accomplished.

Now I allowed myself time to enjoy one selfish thought, the one I had buried most of this weekend. I would see Tess again. I tried to hide my smile. We still had two months to go, but I allowed the thought to drift in my mind as I exited the command post.

Wandering around for a bit after I left the CP, I had a hard time remembering at first where our sleeping tent was located. I found it and grabbed my kit to head for the shower point. After a long shower where I zoned out under a comforting stream of hot water, I wandered back and collapsed into a bed. Someone would find me when the aircraft arrived to take us back to J'bad. Shortly after I finished a thankful prayer and sent my love through the ether to Tess back in New York, I was unconscious.

Reyes shook me awake after a couple of hours, and I packed my gear to leave FOB Joyce. When I arrived on the flight line, my crew was waiting. We all loaded up into a Blackhawk with nothing to say about how, where, or when it flew for the first time in a couple of long, grueling days. We collapsed into the troop seats in the cabin and sat looking at each other with grins on our faces. We had to keep from laughing out loud as the aircraft lifted, providing us with that old familiar feeling in our stomachs.

Kenny and I were on the back wall facing forward. Julia and Capps were strapped in facing us. We just smiled and nodded until the pilots got us clear of the airspace and climbed to a safe altitude. Outside the cabin we watched the familiar structures of FOB Joyce recede and then disappear beneath the clouds. None of us could hold it any longer and we whooped with the unmitigated joy of survival. We sat there screaming things we couldn't hear over the roar of the engines and the clatter of the rotors but what we had to say didn't matter. It was pure emotion, survivor's elation, and we all understood.

We soon got a glimpse of the Cavalry Dustoff flag on our taxiway when the pilots were on approach and exchanged a series of high-fives that missed more than they connected. We were home—or what passed for home on this deployment—and the worst was over for us. We had crossed an important line in our personal and professional lives and survived. We couldn't help believe it was all downhill from here. We had had our "significant emotional event," and it didn't kill us.

We ambled into the Medevac CP and nodded at the Air Force Pararescue pilots who had been covering for us while we flew up at FOB Joyce. They'd been following the action and had some questions about what we'd been through, but none of us were anxious to tell war stories. We gave them a little and then Kenny and I left the CP for the Pilot's Penthouse. Bringloe and Capps shook our hands and then wandered off toward the phones.

I walked beside Kenny toward our rooms. I'd call Tess a little later when the time was right on her end and when I could decide how much to tell her about what we'd been through. I thought about my next assignment as a flight instructor. We'd had no time to get in the training I had wanted.

"Kenny, I guess we won't get in that training…"

"Listen, my man," he said with a grunt. "I think we got all the training you'll need up there in the Watapur." He had grabbed some Valium to help him sleep, soon collapsing in his transient bunk. I didn't see him the rest of the day. I talked a bit with some of my fellow Dustoff aviators. Part of me wouldn't have been shocked to have lost my wings for some of the risks we took together as a team.

I saw my crew again at dinner. Capps was surrounded by his fellow crew-dogs and holding forth with a new degree of respect among his peers. He was no longer the new guy with no combat hoists on his record. David Capps was a man who had seen the elephant and heard the owl. His audience was impressed by a guy who went from no experience to the man who had performed some of the most dangerous hoists they'd ever heard about, in some of the most difficult conditions in history.

We sat down to eat and then SGT Julia Bringloe arrived in her PT gear. She was freshly showered and her legs looked terrible, several shades of black and blue. "Check this out!" she hooted at the assembled flight crews. She did a slow spin and we all got a look at the bruises and gashes that she'd suffered bumping into trees and scraping through obstacles as she rode the hook beneath Dustoff 7-3.

She sat down to eat and ran over our missions in response to questions from her fellow flight medics. She was typically modest, but there was no questioning the facts on record in our command. Julia was fairly beat up from her experiences in the Watapur, but she had rescued 14 soldiers in the worst possible circumstances. We didn't know until after we got home that she'd done most of it with a fractured leg.

After dinner, I got in line for a phone to call Tess. I was so thankful to Jesus Christ to be able to hear her voice. I kept it light. I just said that I was back from the detachment and that I loved her. The truth would come out after I was home and could finally hold her in my arms. She didn't need to sit back in upstate New York with mental images of her husband flying way too close to death. She could tell there was more on my mind but she didn't press for details. I signed off as usual with all my love and wandered back to the Pilot's Penthouse.

Operation *Hammer Down* died down a little while later. Kenny returned with Langa to fly more missions, and soon the operation ended. Another platoon trying to find their way to the LZ for extraction got lost in the fog. Those grunts then found a young goat that led them to the top of the mountain clearing, and they made it out. They adopted him and affectionately named him Dandruff, only to find the Afghani Army soldiers eating him the next day. Eventually, all the soldiers we were supporting were flown out of the Watatpur Valley with all their dead and wounded. Most of the bad guys had been killed or driven out of their bastions, and the command was calling it a success. It was heartening for most of us, but I had an empty place in my heart due to one mission that we missed for reasons beyond our control.

One night while we were waiting for a mission, a female Lieutenant arrived at a base to meet the body of her husband who had been killed in action in the operation. He was the platoon leader from Bravo Company that we'd been scheduled to pick-up. His body had made it back with another crew who finally managed to retrieve him. His wife would accompany First Lieutenant Dimitri del Castillo back home to a hero's burial with honors. He was killed while maneuvering to guide us into the zone to pick up some of his wounded soldiers. The least we could have done was find a way to recover his body, but the situation didn't allow it. I had very few regrets about what we'd done in the Watapur Valley but that was one of them.

While the fight was still going on up there, a lot of other crews flew dicey missions. It never got easier, and outstanding Army Aviators like Alex Langa, Terry O'Brien, Dan Jarc, Travis Bonney, Rich Ernst, Dave Fish, and Rachel Hall

all had close calls flying medevacs. We commiserated when there was time, and swapped experiences, hoping that something we went through would help someone else survive in difficult circumstances. We were all full of praise for our crew chiefs and flight medics, but the tales we told of what Capps and Bringloe did during our turn in the barrel topped them all.

Aaron Michaud got back from his leave which meant that Kenny Brodhead could return to headquarters. I was sitting in the ops area waiting for a mission to drop when he walked by me on his way to catch his ride. Kenny paused to shift his bags, and looked in my direction without looking me in the eyes. I looked up at his grin beneath that mustache.

"It was special, Erik."

EPILOGUE

CHIEF WARRANT OFFICER 4 Kenny Brodhead returned to Afghanistan again the next year. Specialist David Capps joined the Nebraska National Guard and is still serving with them today. I soon left Fort Drum for Fort Rucker to begin training as a UH-60 instructor pilot. Sergeant Julia Bringloe was reunited with her son in Hawaii. Julia also deployed with Kenny to Afghanistan, serving as the senior flight instructor for all the back-seaters in the company. We stayed in intermittent contact, mostly just asking and answering questions about our personal lives. We talked about what happened that one long weekend in the Watapur Valley, but we also tried not to talk about it at the same time. I tried to shelve it all and focus on teaching young officers to fly Army helicopters.

When I wasn't concentrating on duty concerns and the details of flying and teaching, I couldn't seem to avoid a series of nagging questions. Had I done everything I could? If so, why hadn't we been able to rescue everyone who needed it up in that Afghan valley? Was there something more I could have done as a pilot in command? Mostly, I was bothered by my failure to save one particular man from those dangerous and hotly contested hillsides.

Then one day, the clouds began to dissipate after I got a call from Julia Bringloe.

"Sabby, I'm getting married!" She sounded elated and bubbly—much different from the serious, dedicated Flight Medic I'd left when Tess and I moved to Fort Rucker.

"Who's the lucky guy?" I waved Tess over to listen in on the call.

"One of my patients," she said with a laugh. "He's one of the guys that I pulled out of a firefight. He had a few gunshot wounds and I plugged them up while we got him to the hospital. He hunted me down to thank me—and we just fell in love!"

"When's the wedding?"

"March—the same day we first met."

Somehow, Julia's good news, a happy ending to the experience in Afghanistan for her and a soldier that she'd saved, lifted my spirits. He was a great guy and she deserved to be happy. He even got into flight school, with hopes of someday becoming a Dustoff pilot himself. I began to recuperate. In November, a year after we had returned from the combat zone, Newsweek Magazine ran an article that featured me and my crew and talked about our medevac missions. A lot of people—soldiers and civilians—would ask me about it. I mostly shrugged off the embarrassing attention. One day I got a letter from none other than Prodigal 1-7, SFC Niobel Santos, the NCO who served with Bravo Company during the brutal battle near the *qalat* and was there when Lieutenant del Castillo was killed. Here's what he had to say:

"Your crew was great and without you guys doing what you did I would have lost more of my Soldiers. There was truly nothing we could have done for Dimitri to save him. He was an amazing person and one of my best friends. I can honestly say that he is one of the best humans I've met in my life. Whether through good times or bad times, God is always with us and he was for the days we were on that mission. It could have been much worse. I would not want any other crew watching my back or coming to get me if I was wounded or if I ever found myself in that situation again. I ask myself a lot why God didn't choose me that day instead of Del, but I know I'm a better person because of him, and I live everyday trying to emulate the goodness that he embodied."

The rest of the clouds disappeared when I read that, and I found myself comfortable with myself and my efforts for the first time. It was time to give my own perspective on the experience.

I got started by writing five words: This story is for heroes.

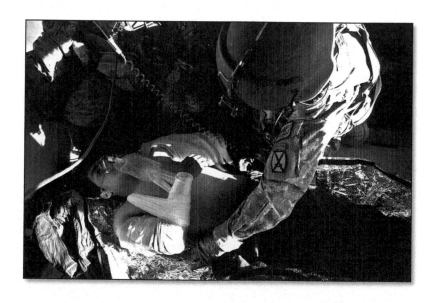

PHOTO CREDITS

Pg. 14: "Ready For Taxi." Buckley AFB, CO Unit: C co/2-135 GSAB, CO-ARNG, UH-60A (83-23908) is ready for taxi in this time-exposure shot, September 7, 2008. Copyright © Marc Belo.

Pg. 44: Photo of SGT Johnny Reyes at Jalalabad Army Airfield C Co. 3-10 GSAB, 4th Platoon MEDEVAC Command Post, September 21, 2010. Copyright © CPT Drew Wilson.

Pg. 63: "On The Porch" by Brian Cammack. Members of C Co. 3-10 GSAB, 4th Platoon at FOB Fenty, Jalalabad, Afghanistan, April 2, 2011. Copyright © Brian Cammack.

Pg. 81: CAMP MARMAL, Afghanistan-- A pararescue airman lowers to the ground while latched on to the jungle penetrator of an aircraft hoist during. Photo by SSG Joe Armas.

Pg. 104: From the helmet camera of SSG Brian Cammack, during a MEDEVAC hoist mission supporting the 101st Airborne in the Kunar Valley, Afghanistan, March 22, 2011.

Pg. 119: Photo of CW2 Erik Sabiston by Mitch Weise on February 15, 2011 north of Ghazni Province Afghanistan. Copyright © Mitch Weise.

Pg. 132: Dustoff 7-3 as photographed by 1LT Dimitri del Castillo, 2-35 INF, Operation *Hammerdown II*, June 25th 2011, Eastern Watapur Valley, Afghanistan. Copyright © the estate of Dimitri del Castillo.

Pg. 148: CW2 Erik Sabiston running up 944, photo by SPC David Capps, early on June 25th 2011, FOB Fenty, Jalalabad, Afghanistan, Operation *Hammerdown II*. Copyright © David Capps.

Pg. 155: "Angel Overwatch" by David Burson, Faryab Province RC North, FOB Meymanah, August 15 2011. Copyright © David Burson.

Pg. 176: David Capps as photographed by Erik Sabiston on June 27, 2011, over the Kunar Valley after surviving Operation *Hammerdown II*, Afghanistan. Copyright © Erik Sabiston.

Pg. 186: Logar Province, Afghanistan. Dustoff mission as photographed by Harry Sanna on March 20, 2011. Copyright © Harry Sanna.

Pg. 196: Photo of SGT Julia Bringloe riding the hoist in the Kunar Valley, June 19, 2015. Copyright © Julia Bringloe.

Pg. 211: "Through The Mist." Photo by David Burson on April 22, 2012, Faryab Province, RC North, FOB Meymanah. Copyright © David Burson.

Pg. 220: CW4 Kenny Brodhead as photographed by Erik Sabiston on June 27, 2011, over the Kunar Valley after surviving Operation *Hammerdown II*, Afghanistan. Copyright © Erik Sabiston.

Pg. 223: Logar Province. Dustoff mission as photographed by Harry Sanna on March 20, 2011. Copyright © Harry Sanna.

About the Author: Erik Sabiston as photographed by Platon in New York City on Oct, 30, 2012, for the Newsweek Heroes Issue. Copyright © Platon.

Every effort has been made to acknowledge correctly the source and/or copyright holders of these illustrations, and Warriors Publishing Group apologizes for any unintentional errors or omissions, which will be corrected in future editions.

ABOUT THE AUTHOR

ERIK SABISTON grew up in the Blue Ridge Mountains of Virginia before winding up living off the grid in the redwoods of Northern California. Naturally restless, he moved from one job to another working as a door-to-door salesman, music teacher, and even a butcher, until he eventually found his calling as a Soldier. He led his helicopter crew during a series of miraculous rescues  on one of the most dangerous operations in the history of the war in Afghanistan.

Erik also speaks nationwide at conferences, schools, and events, inspiring audiences to harness the power of faith and teamwork to push themselves beyond their own limits, survive the unthinkable, and achieve the impossible.

He currently teaches the next generation of aviators to fly and fight in the UH-60 Blackhawk helicopter. Home is wherever the Army sends him and his wife Tess—who still teases him about his fear of heights.

With love, respect and gratitude to my heroes, Kenny, Julia and David. Special thanks to Dale and Julia for many nights of pizza, as well as Ron Tsolis, my favorite aviator and extra pair of eyes.

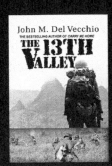

1-16

CPSIA information can be obtained
at www.ICGtesting.com
Printed in the USA
LVOW01s1549200116
471541LV00020B/838/P